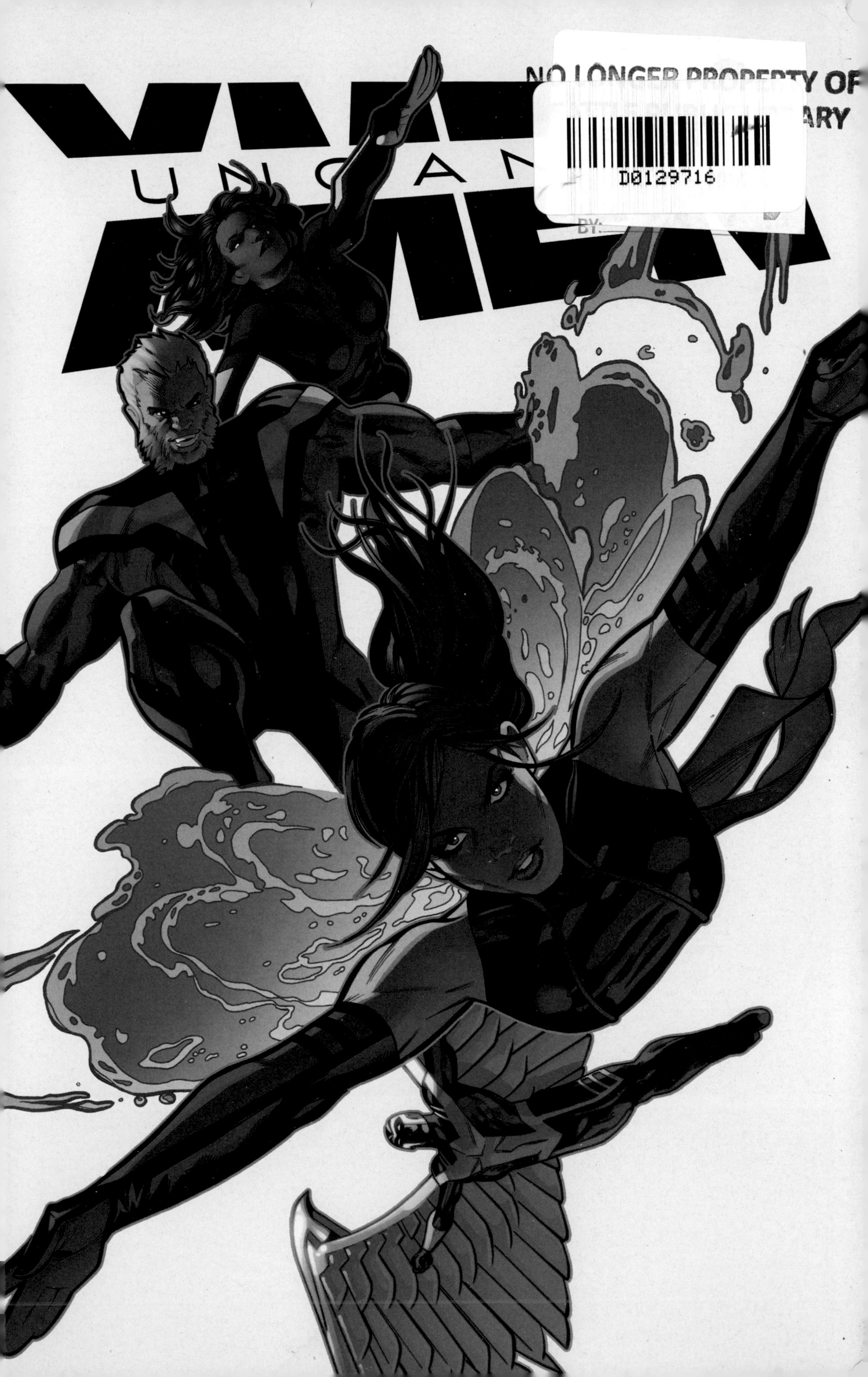

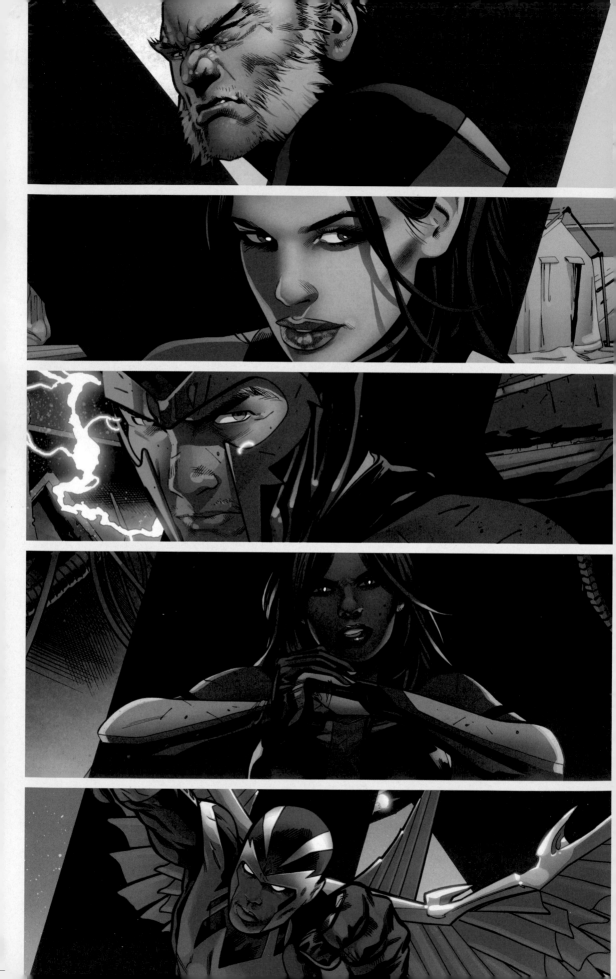

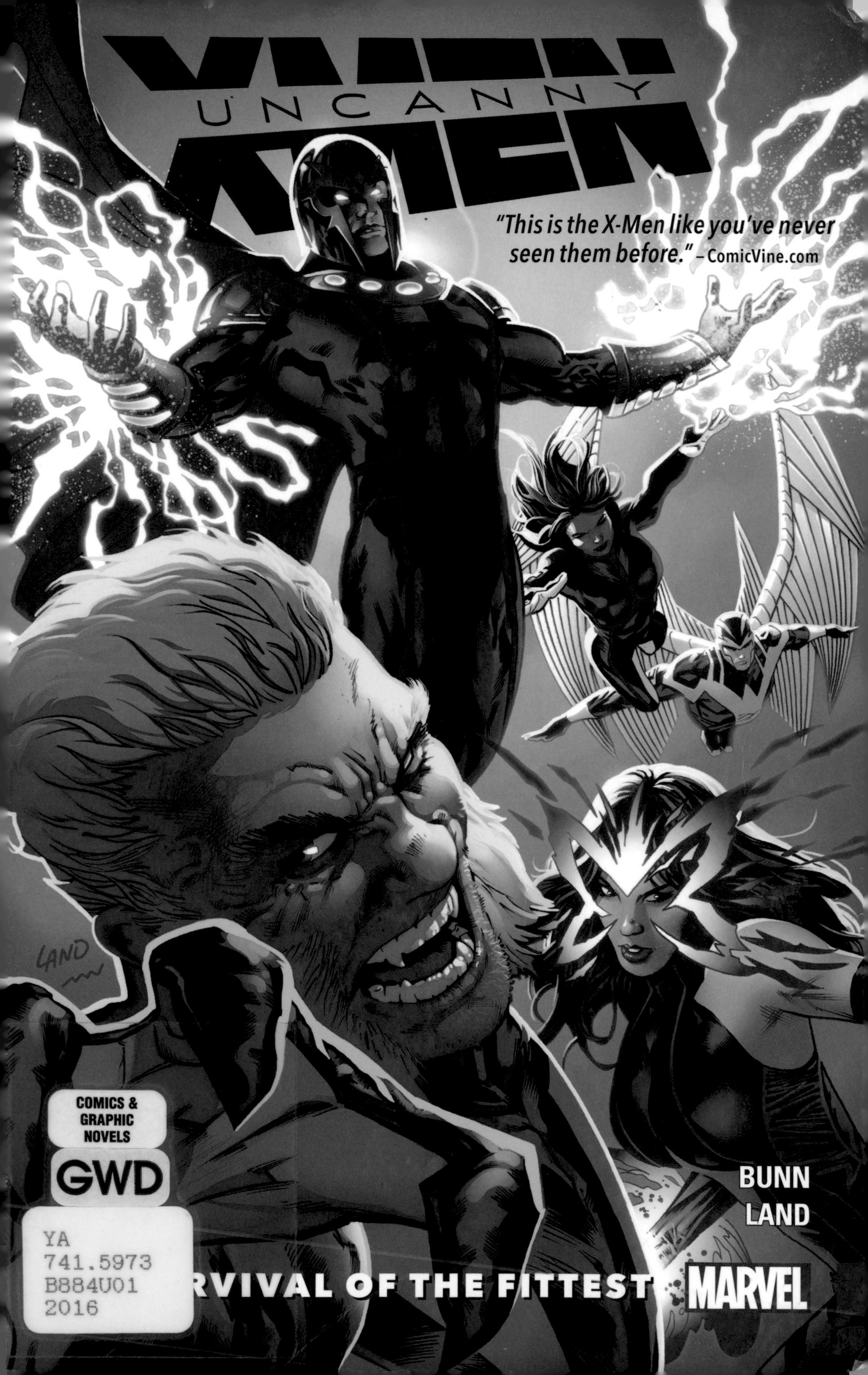
UNCANNY
"This is the X-Men like you've never seen them before." – ComicVine.com
LAND
BUNN
LAND
RVIVAL OF THE FITTEST
MARVEL

Collected Editions

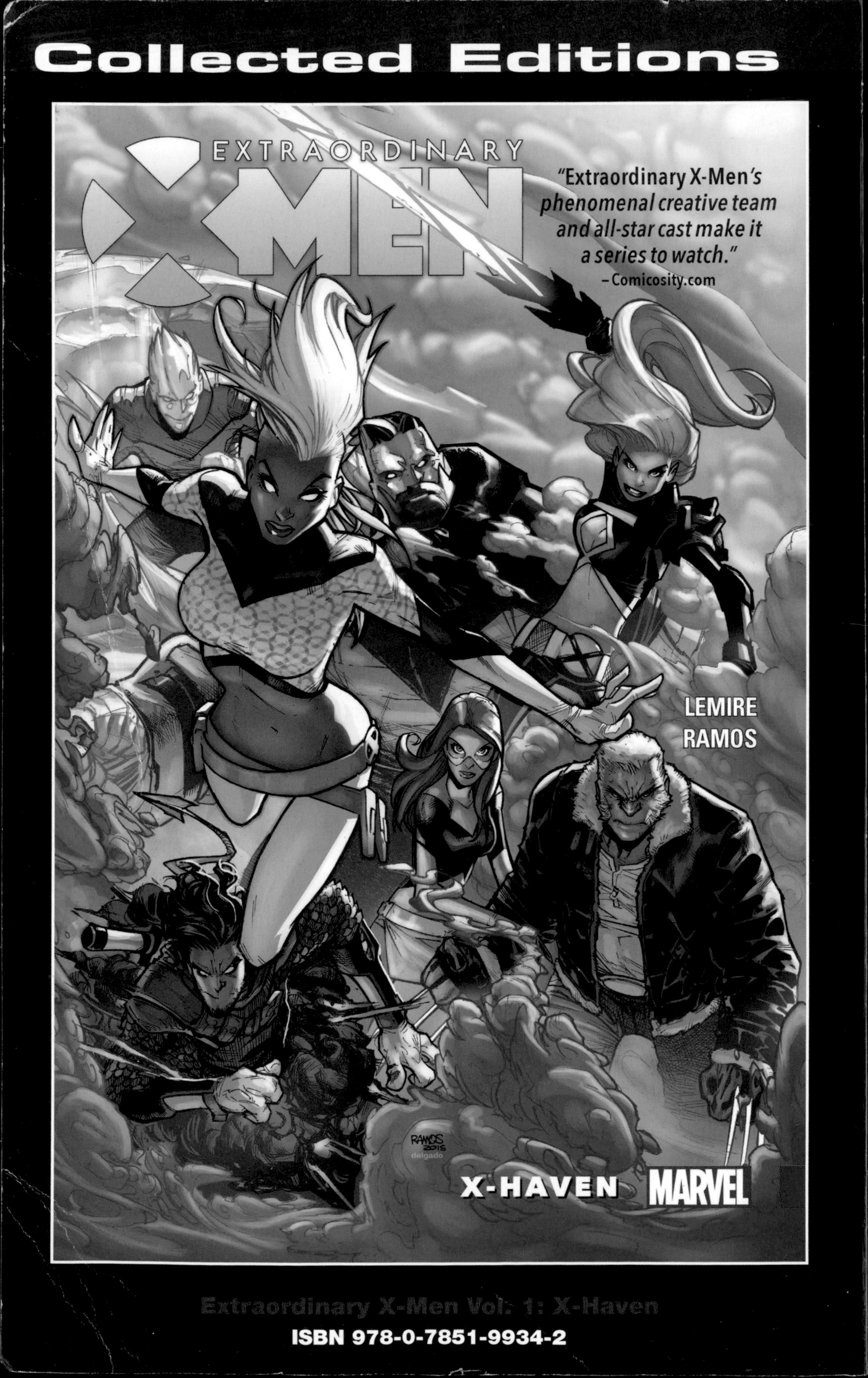
EXTRAORDINARY
X-MEN
"Extraordinary X-Men's phenomenal creative team and all-star cast make it a series to watch."
– Comicosity.com
LEMIRE
RAMOS
X-HAVEN
MARVEL

Extraordinary X-Men Vol. 1: X-Haven

ISBN 978-0-7851-9934-2

THE X-MEN HAVE ALWAYS PROTECTED A WORLD THAT HATES AND FEARS THEM, BUT AS ANTI-MUTANT SENTIMENT REACHES A FEVER PITCH, THE EARTH'S REMAINING MUTANTS FIND THEMSELVES NOT JUST FIGHTING FOR PEACE, BUT FIGHTING FOR THEIR LIVES. AS THE SITUATION BECOMES INCREASINGLY DIRE, THE TRUTH BECOMES EVIDENT: BIGGER THREATS REQUIRE MORE THREATENING X-MEN...

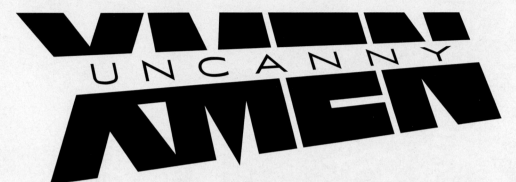

UNCANNY X-MEN

SURVIVAL OF THE FITTEST

CULLEN BUNN
WRITER

GREG LAND
PENCILER

JAY LEISTEN
INKER

NOLAN WOODARD
COLORIST

VC'S JOE CARAMAGNA
LETTERER

GREG LAND, JAY LEISTEN & NOLAN WOODARD
COVER ART

CHRISTINA HARRINGTON
ASSISTANT EDITOR

DANIEL KETCHUM
EDITOR

MARK PANICCIA
X-MEN GROUP EDITOR

X-MEN CREATED BY *STAN LEE & JACK KIRBY*

COLLECTION EDITOR: ***JENNIFER GRÜNWALD***
ASSOCIATE EDITOR: ***SARAH BRUNSTAD***
ASSOCIATE MANAGING EDITOR: ***ALEX STARBUCK***
EDITOR, SPECIAL PROJECTS: ***MARK D. BEAZLEY***
VP, PRODUCTION & SPECIAL PROJECTS: ***JEFF YOUNGQUIST***
SVP PRINT, SALES & MARKETING: ***DAVID GABRIEL***
BOOK DESIGNER: ***JAY BOWEN***

EDITOR IN CHIEF: ***AXEL ALONSO***
CHIEF CREATIVE OFFICER: ***JOE QUESADA***
PUBLISHER: ***DAN BUCKLEY***
EXECUTIVE PRODUCER: ***ALAN FINE***

UNCANNY X-MEN: SUPERIOR VOL. 1 — SURVIVAL OF THE FITTEST. Contains material originally published in magazine form as UNCANNY X-MEN #1-5. First printing 2016. ISBN# 978-0-7851-9607-5. Published by MARVEL WORLDWIDE, INC., a subsidiary of MARVEL ENTERTAINMENT, LLC. OFFICE OF PUBLICATION: 135 West 50th Street, New York, NY 10020. **Printed in Canada.** ALAN FINE, President, Marvel Entertainment; DAN BUCKLEY, President, TV, Publishing & Brand Management; JOE QUESADA, Chief Creative Officer; TOM BREVOORT, SVP of Publishing; DAVID BOGART, SVP of Business Affairs & Operations, Publishing & Partnership; C.B. CEBULSKI, VP of Brand Management & Development, Asia; DAVID GABRIEL, SVP of Sales & Marketing, Publishing; JEFF YOUNGQUIST, VP of Production & Special Projects; DAN CARR, Executive Director of Publishing Technology; ALEX MORALES, Director of Publishing Operations; SUSAN CRESPI, Production Manager; STAN LEE, Chairman Emeritus. For information regarding advertising in Marvel Comics or on Marvel.com, please contact Vit DeBellis, Integrated Sales Manager, at vdebellis@marvel.com. For Marvel subscription inquiries, please call 888-511-5480. **Manufactured between 5/6/2016 and 6/13/2016 by SOLISCO PRINTERS, SCOTT, QC, CANADA.**

10 9 8 7 6 5 4 3 2 1

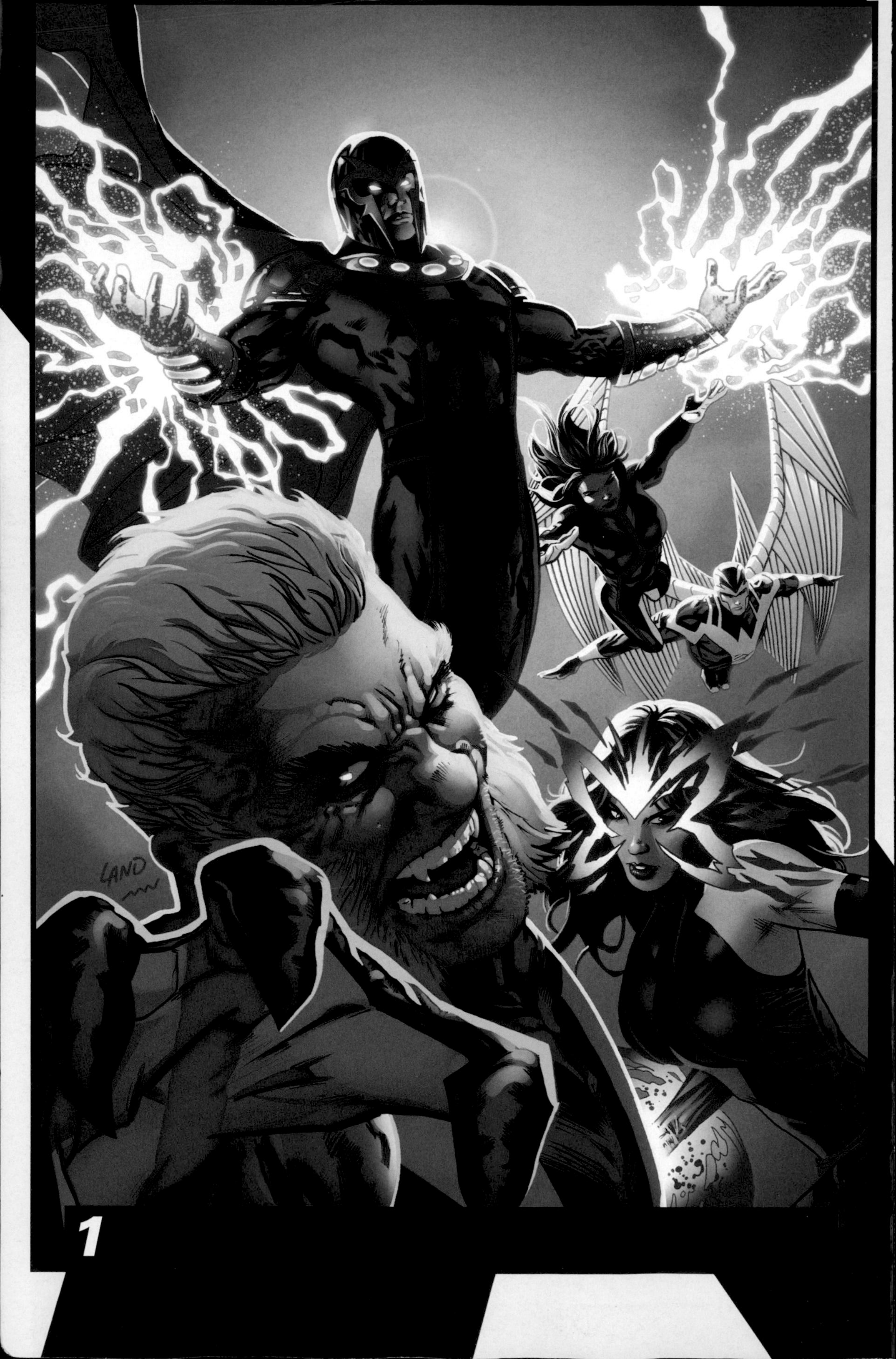
LAND

1

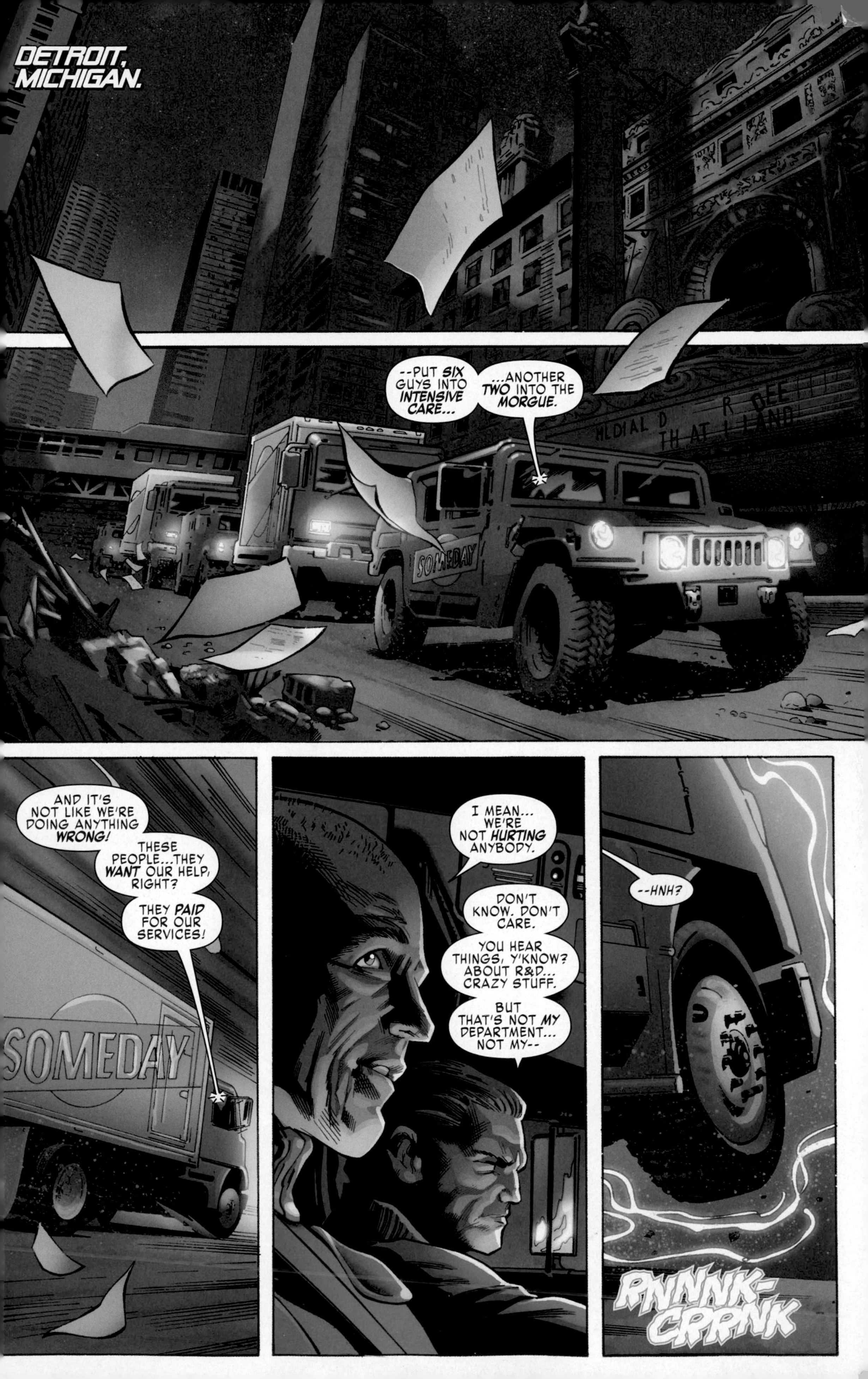

DETROIT, MICHIGAN.
--PUT SIX GUYS INTO INTENSIVE CARE...
...ANOTHER TWO INTO THE MORGUE.
SOMEDAY
AND IT'S NOT LIKE WE'RE DOING ANYTHING WRONG!
THESE PEOPLE...THEY WANT OUR HELP, RIGHT?
THEY PAID FOR OUR SERVICES!
SOMEDAY
I MEAN... WE'RE NOT HURTING ANYBODY.
DON'T KNOW. DON'T CARE.
YOU HEAR THINGS, Y'KNOW? ABOUT R&D... CRAZY STUFF.
BUT THAT'S NOT MY DEPARTMENT... NOT MY--
--HNH?
RNNNK-CRRNK

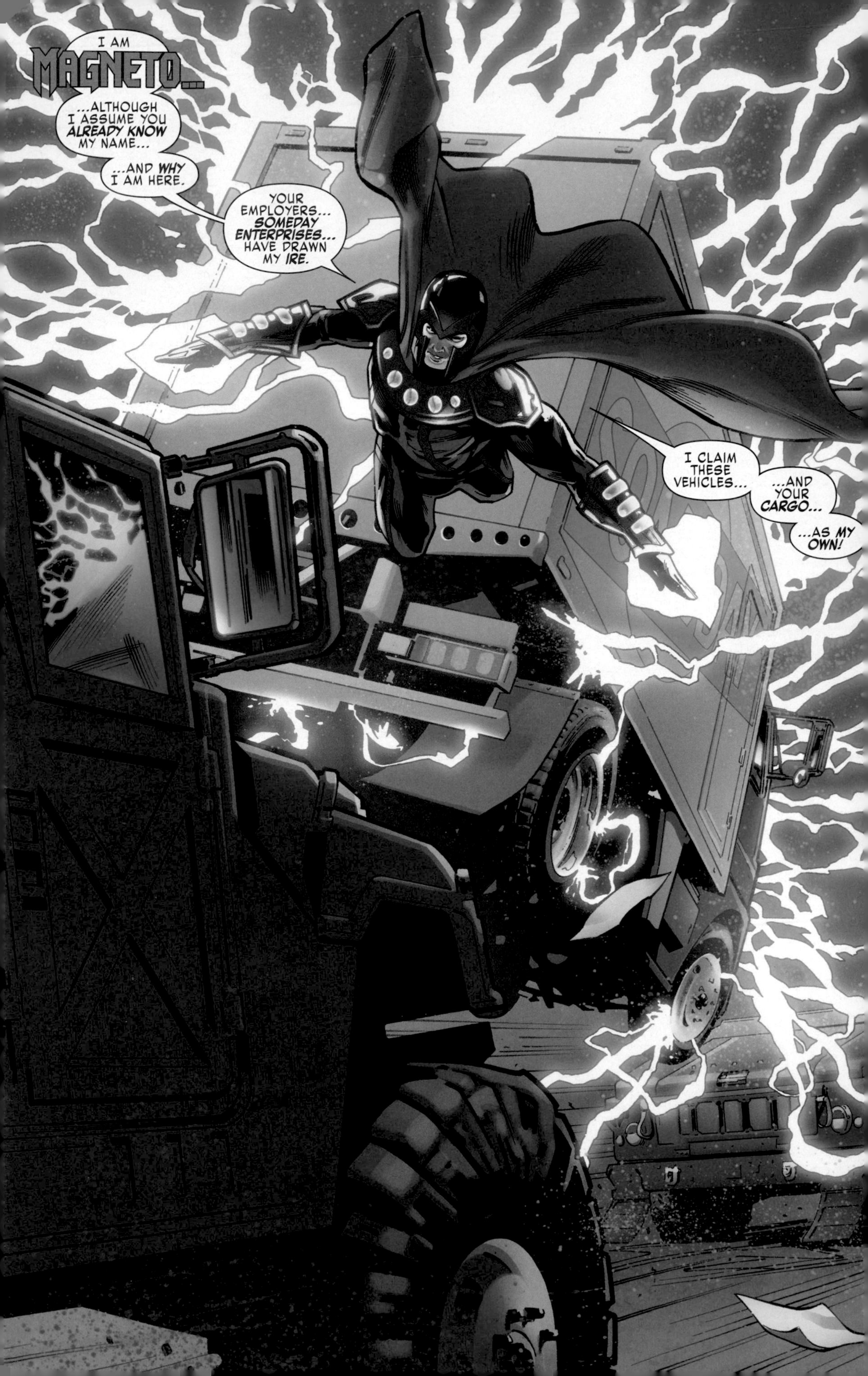
I AM MAGNETO...
...ALTHOUGH I ASSUME YOU ALREADY KNOW MY NAME...
...AND WHY I AM HERE.
YOUR EMPLOYERS... SOMEDAY ENTERPRISES... HAVE DRAWN MY IRE.
I CLAIM THESE VEHICLES...
...AND YOUR CARGO...
...AS MY OWN!

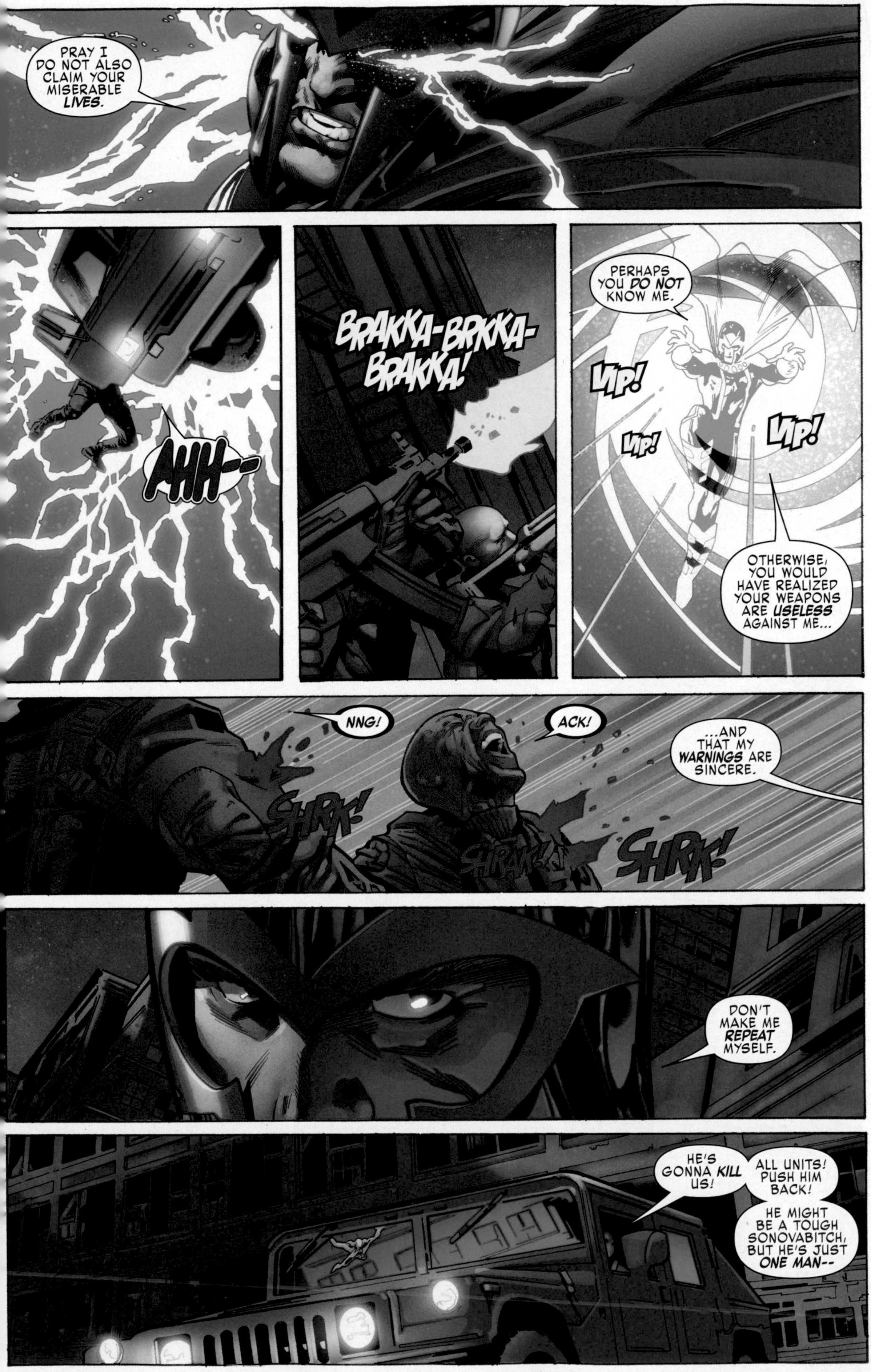
PRAY I DO NOT ALSO CLAIM YOUR MISERABLE LIVES.
AHH--
BRAKKA-BRKKA-BRAKKA!
PERHAPS YOU DO NOT KNOW ME.
VIP!
VIP!
VIP!
OTHERWISE, YOU WOULD HAVE REALIZED YOUR WEAPONS ARE USELESS AGAINST ME...
NNG!
ACK!
...AND THAT MY WARNINGS ARE SINCERE.
SHRK!
SHRAK!
SHRK!
DON'T MAKE ME REPEAT MYSELF.
HE'S GONNA KILL US!
ALL UNITS! PUSH HIM BACK!
HE MIGHT BE A TOUGH SONOVABITCH, BUT HE'S JUST ONE MAN--

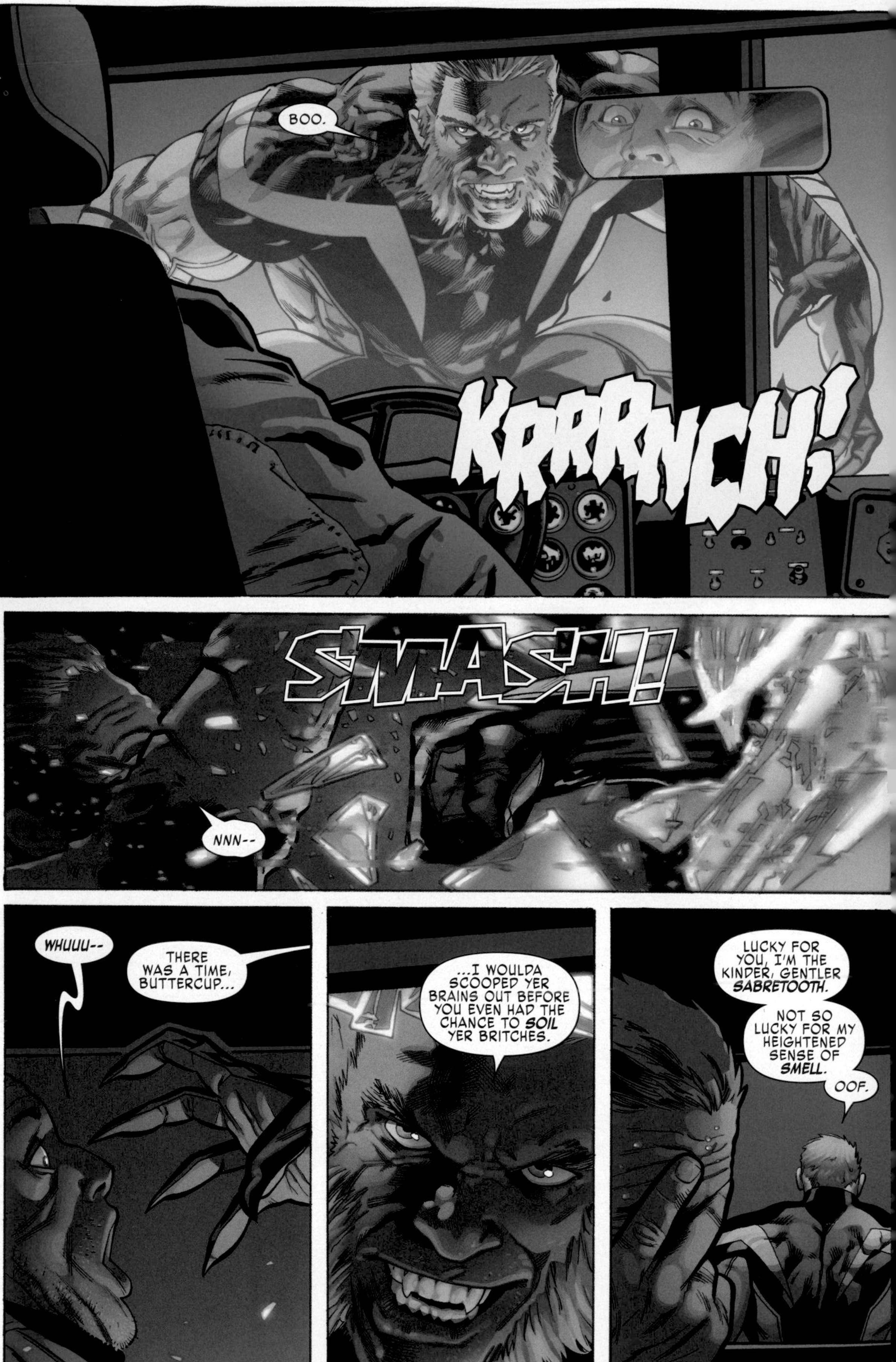
BOO.
KRRRNCH!
SMASH!
NNN--
WHUUU--
THERE WAS A TIME, BUTTERCUP...
...I WOULDA SCOOPED YER BRAINS OUT BEFORE YOU EVEN HAD THE CHANCE TO SOIL YER BRITCHES.
LUCKY FOR YOU, I'M THE KINDER, GENTLER SABRETOOTH.
NOT SO LUCKY FOR MY HEIGHTENED SENSE OF SMELL.
OOF.

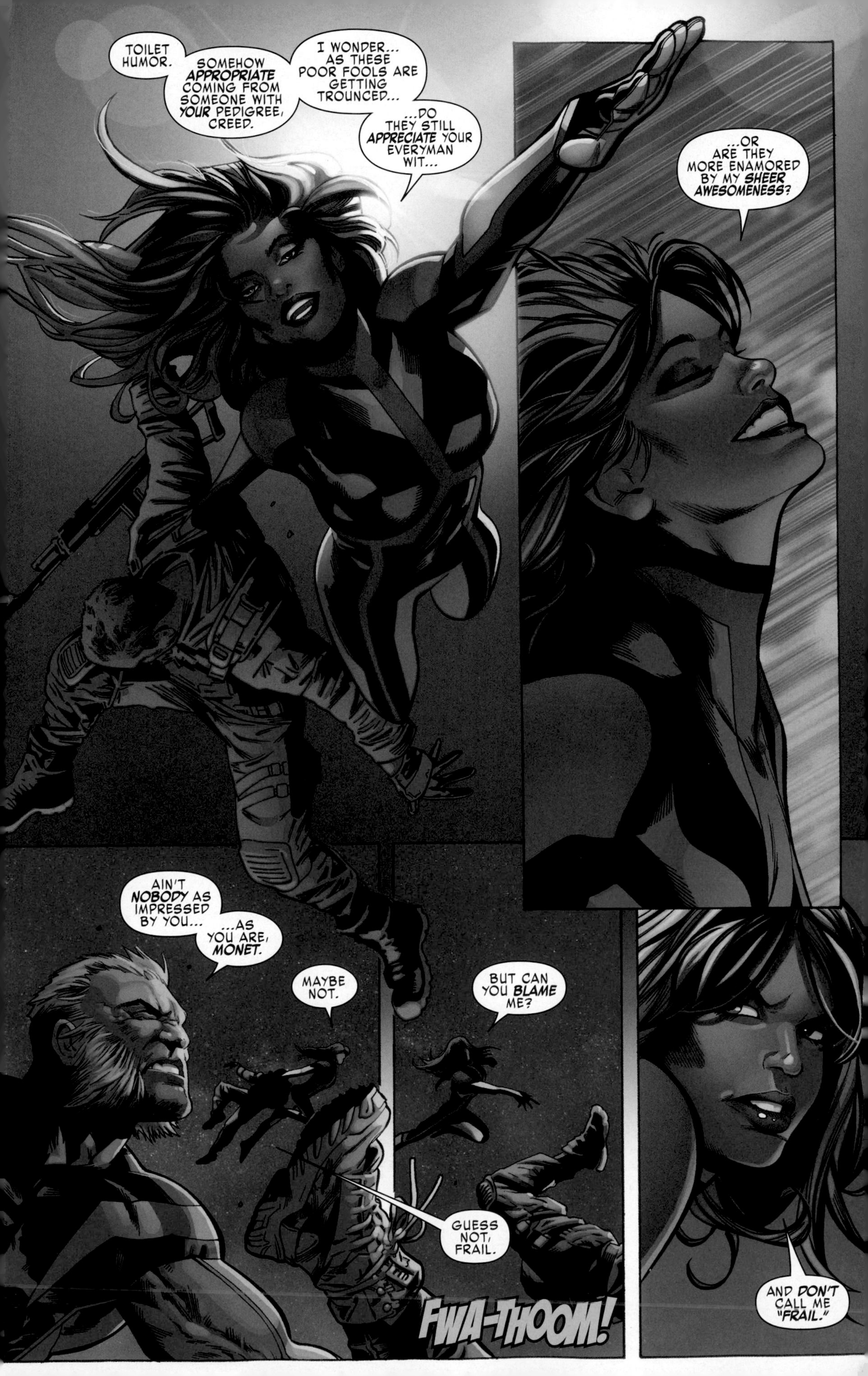
TOILET HUMOR.
SOMEHOW APPROPRIATE COMING FROM SOMEONE WITH YOUR PEDIGREE, CREED.
I WONDER... AS THESE POOR FOOLS ARE GETTING TROUNCED...
...DO THEY STILL APPRECIATE YOUR EVERYMAN WIT...
...OR ARE THEY MORE ENAMORED BY MY SHEER AWESOMENESS?
AIN'T NOBODY AS IMPRESSED BY YOU...
...AS YOU ARE, MONET.
MAYBE NOT.
BUT CAN YOU BLAME ME?
GUESS NOT, FRAIL.
FWA-THOOM!
AND DON'T CALL ME "FRAIL."

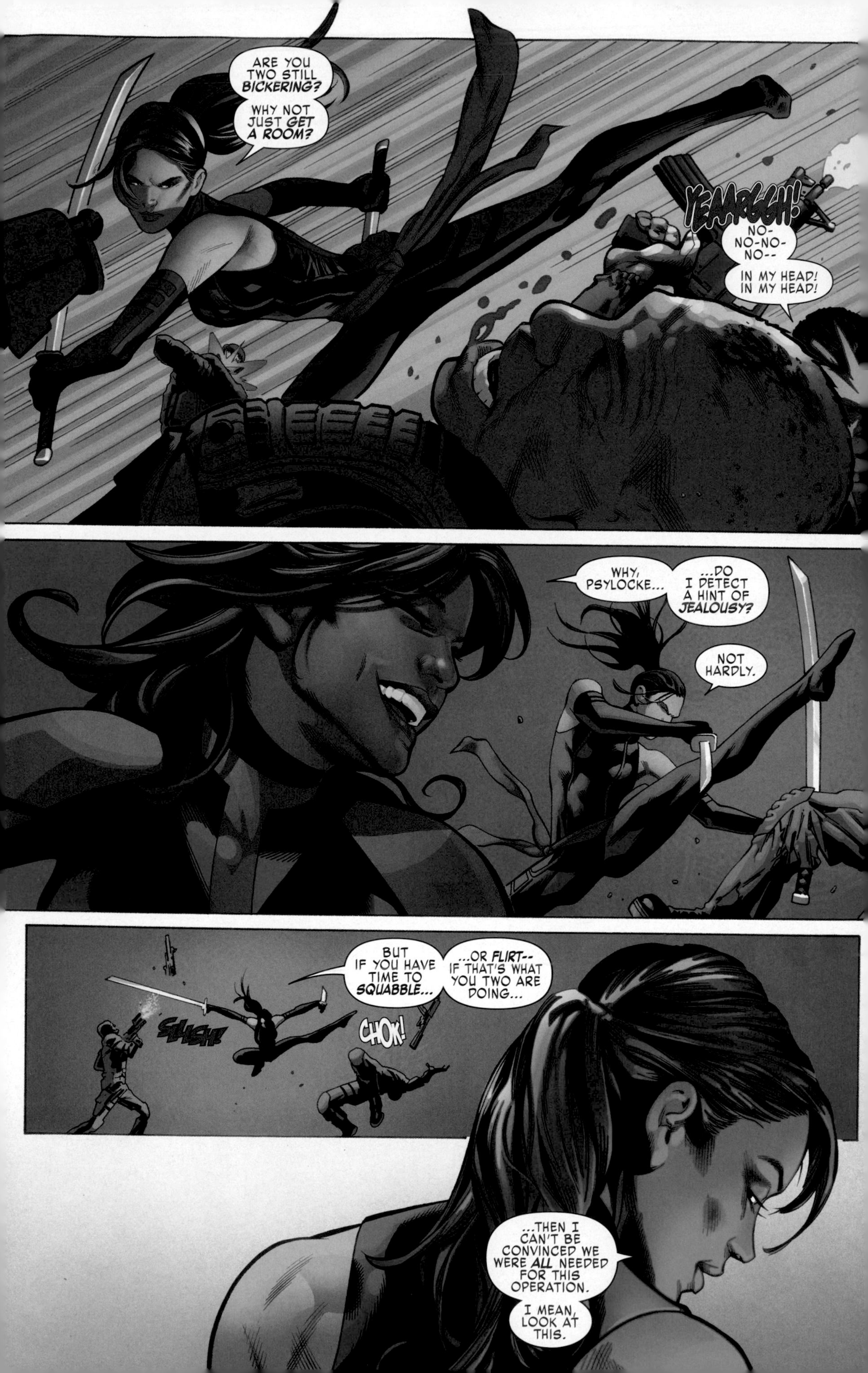
ARE YOU TWO STILL BICKERING?
WHY NOT JUST GET A ROOM?
YEAARGGH!
NO-NO-NO-NO--
IN MY HEAD! IN MY HEAD!
WHY, PSYLOCKE...
...DO I DETECT A HINT OF JEALOUSY?
NOT HARDLY.
BUT IF YOU HAVE TIME TO SQUABBLE...
...OR FLIRT-- IF THAT'S WHAT YOU TWO ARE DOING...
SLISH!
CHOK!
...THEN I CAN'T BE CONVINCED WE WERE ALL NEEDED FOR THIS OPERATION.
I MEAN, LOOK AT THIS.

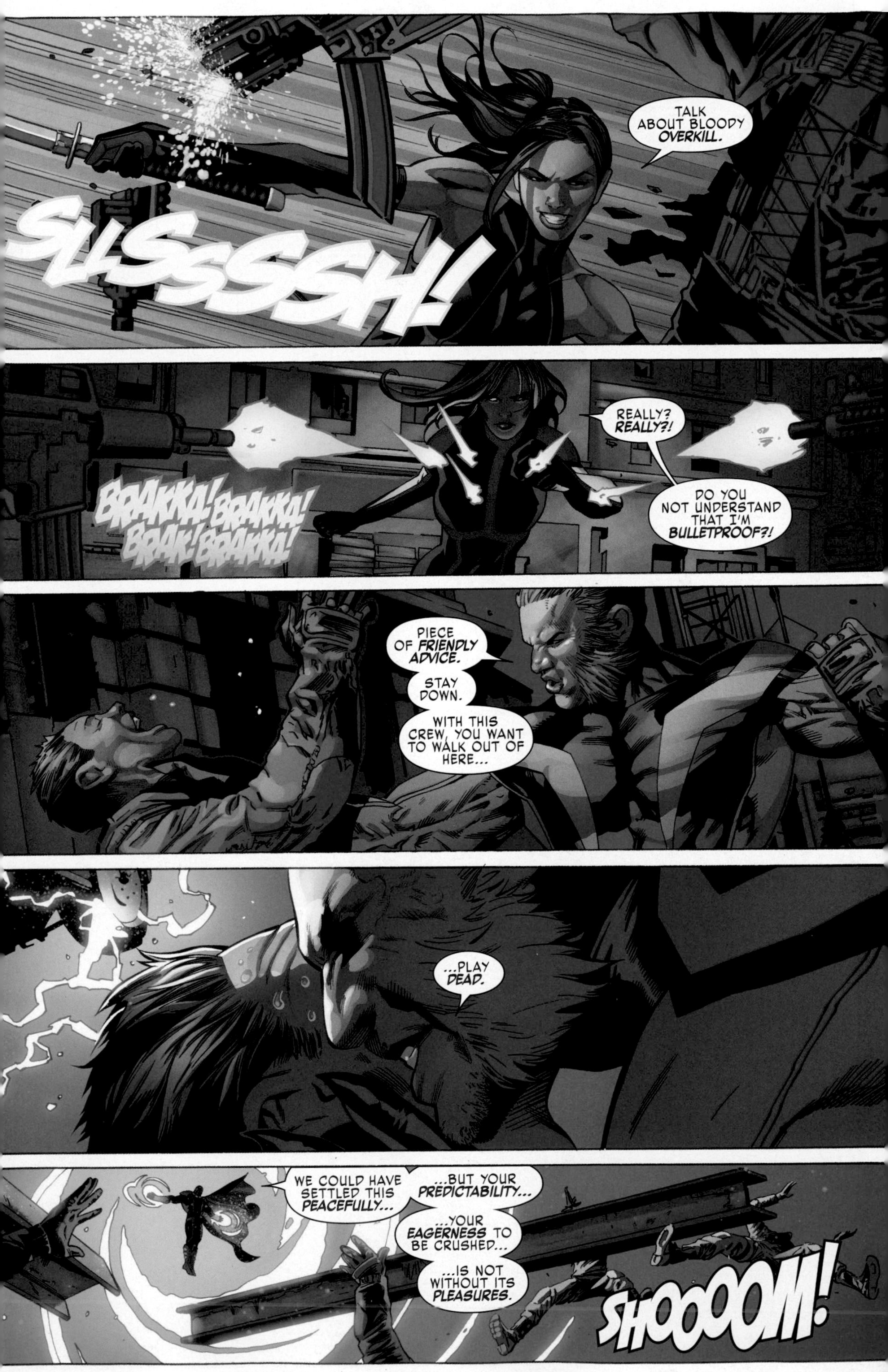
TALK ABOUT BLOODY OVERKILL.
SLISSSSH!
REALLY? REALLY?!
DO YOU NOT UNDERSTAND THAT I'M BULLETPROOF?!
BRAKKA! BRAKKA! BRAK! BRAKKA!
PIECE OF FRIENDLY ADVICE.
STAY DOWN.
WITH THIS CREW, YOU WANT TO WALK OUT OF HERE...
...PLAY DEAD.
WE COULD HAVE SETTLED THIS PEACEFULLY...
...BUT YOUR PREDICTABILITY...
...YOUR EAGERNESS TO BE CRUSHED...
...IS NOT WITHOUT ITS PLEASURES.
SHOOOOM!

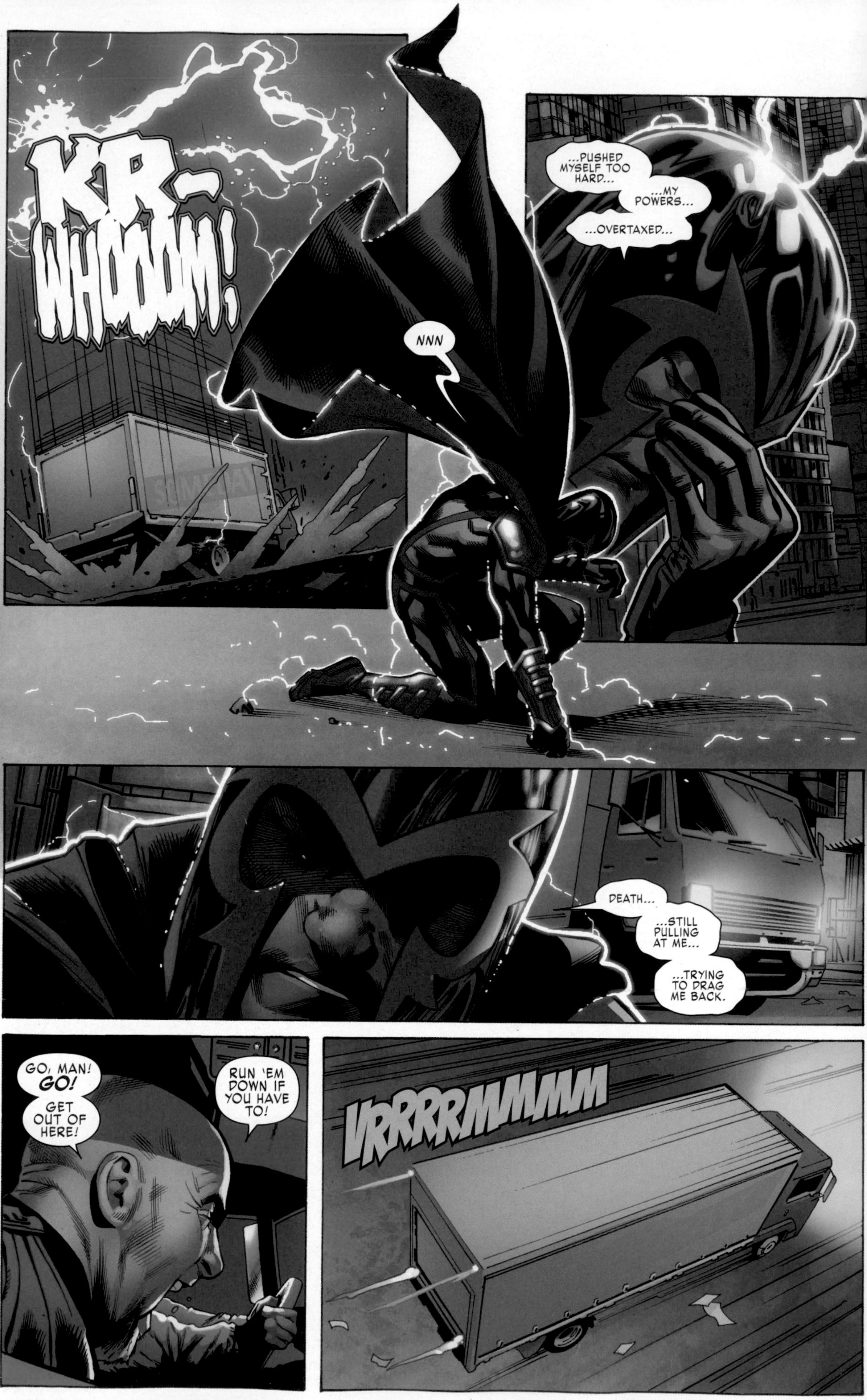

KR-WHOOOM!
...PUSHED MYSELF TOO HARD...
...MY POWERS...
...OVERTAXED...
NNN
DEATH...
...STILL PULLING AT ME...
...TRYING TO DRAG ME BACK.
GO, MAN! GO!
GET OUT OF HERE!
RUN 'EM DOWN IF YOU HAVE TO!
VRRRRMMMMM

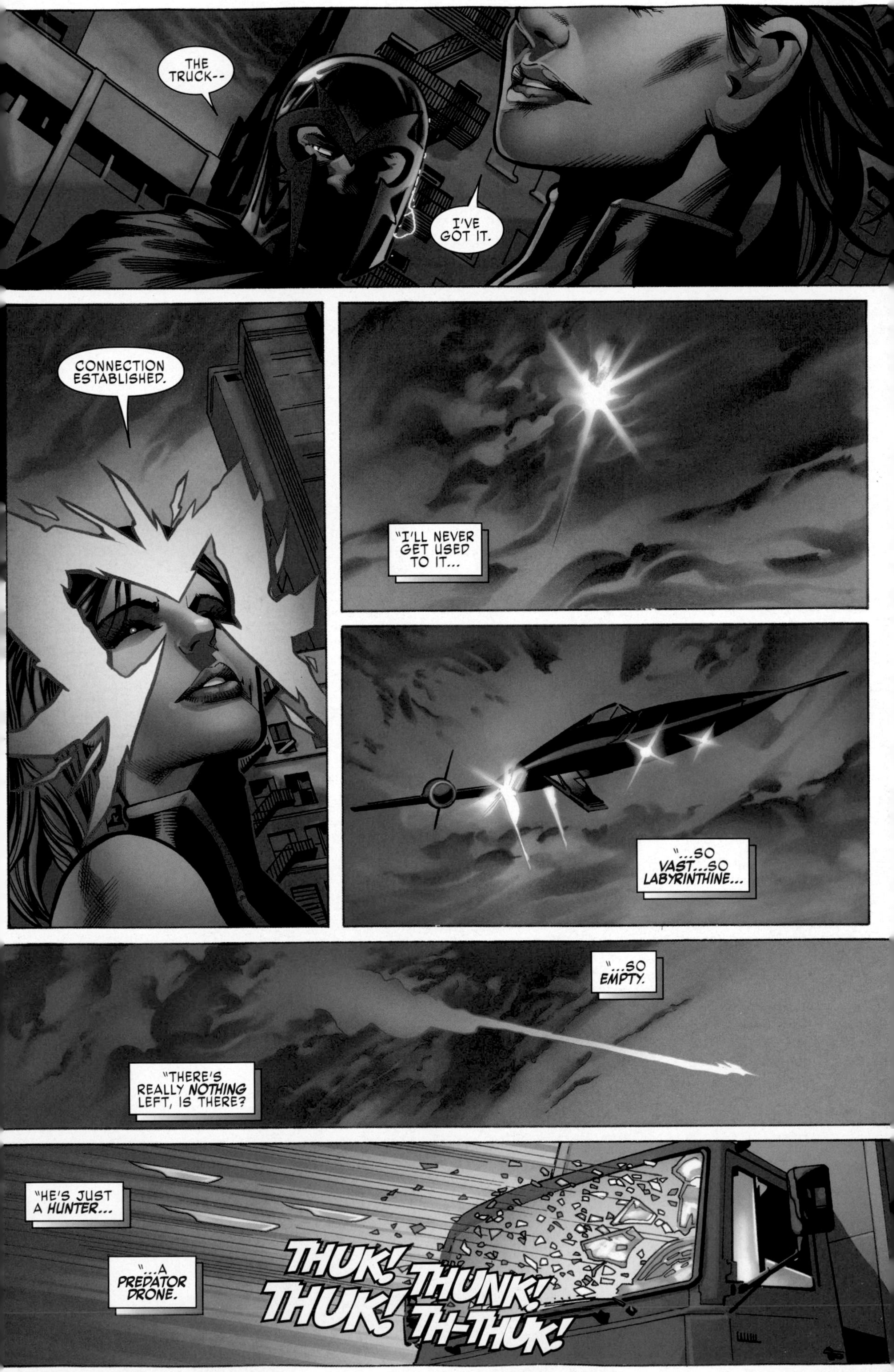
THE TRUCK--
I'VE GOT IT.
CONNECTION ESTABLISHED.
"I'LL NEVER GET USED TO IT...
"...SO VAST...SO LABYRINTHINE...
"...SO EMPTY.
"THERE'S REALLY NOTHING LEFT, IS THERE?
"HE'S JUST A HUNTER...
"...A PREDATOR DRONE.
THUK! THUK! THUNK! TH-THUK!

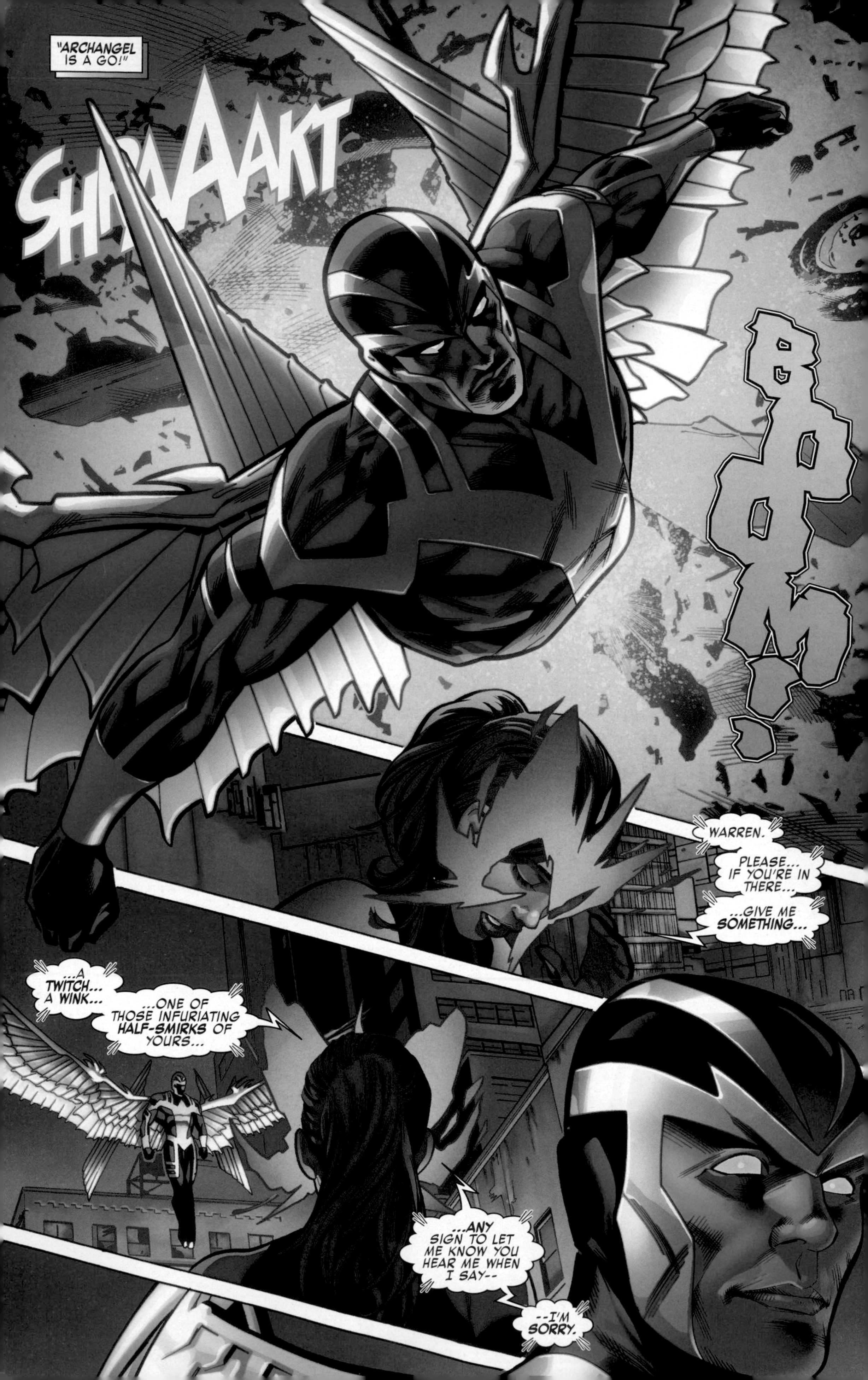
"ARCHANGEL IS A GO!"
SHRAAAKT
BOOM
WARREN.
PLEASE... IF YOU'RE IN THERE...
...GIVE ME **SOMETHING...**
...A **TWITCH...** A **WINK...**
...ONE OF THOSE INFURIATING **HALF-SMIRKS** OF YOURS...
...**ANY** SIGN TO LET ME KNOW YOU HEAR ME WHEN I SAY--
--I'M **SORRY.**

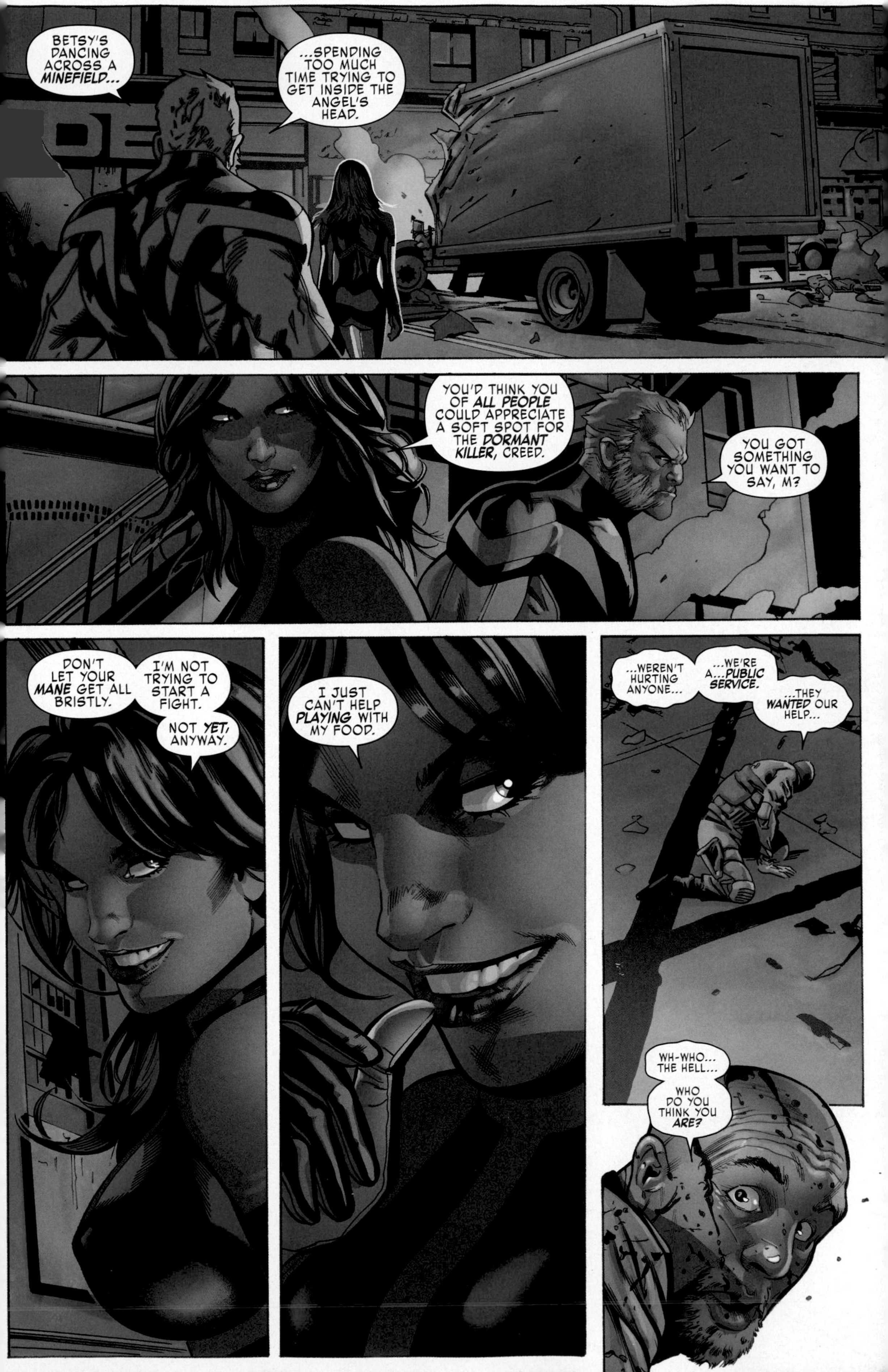
BETSY'S DANCING ACROSS A *MINEFIELD*...
...SPENDING TOO MUCH TIME TRYING TO GET INSIDE THE ANGEL'S HEAD.
YOU'D THINK YOU OF *ALL PEOPLE* COULD APPRECIATE A SOFT SPOT FOR THE *DORMANT KILLER*, CREED.
YOU GOT SOMETHING YOU WANT TO SAY, M?
DON'T LET YOUR *MANE* GET ALL BRISTLY.
I'M NOT TRYING TO START A FIGHT.
NOT *YET*, ANYWAY.
I JUST CAN'T HELP *PLAYING* WITH MY FOOD.
...WEREN'T HURTING ANYONE...
...WE'RE A...*PUBLIC SERVICE.*
...THEY *WANTED* OUR HELP...
WH-WHO... THE HELL...
WHO DO YOU THINK YOU *ARE?*

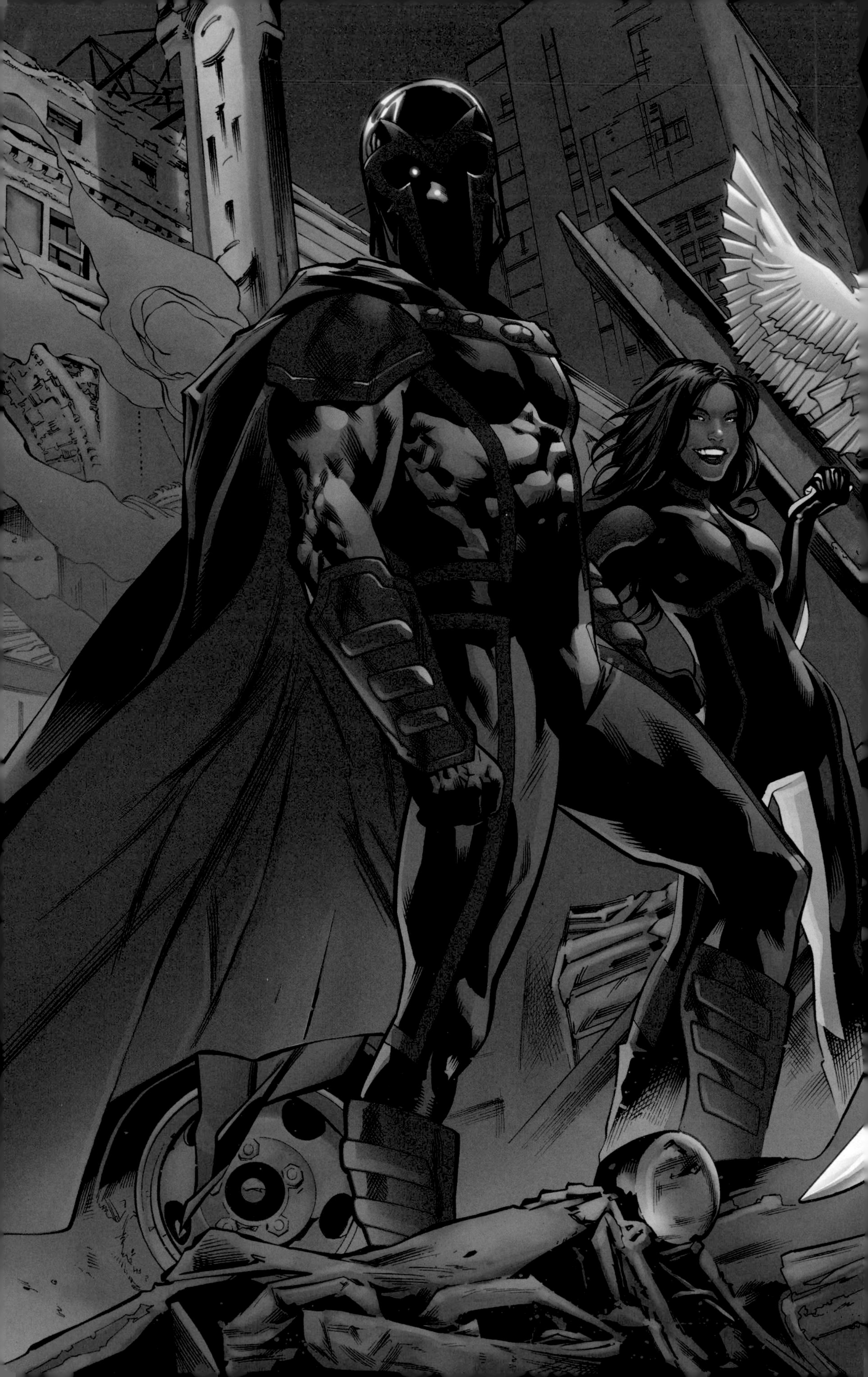

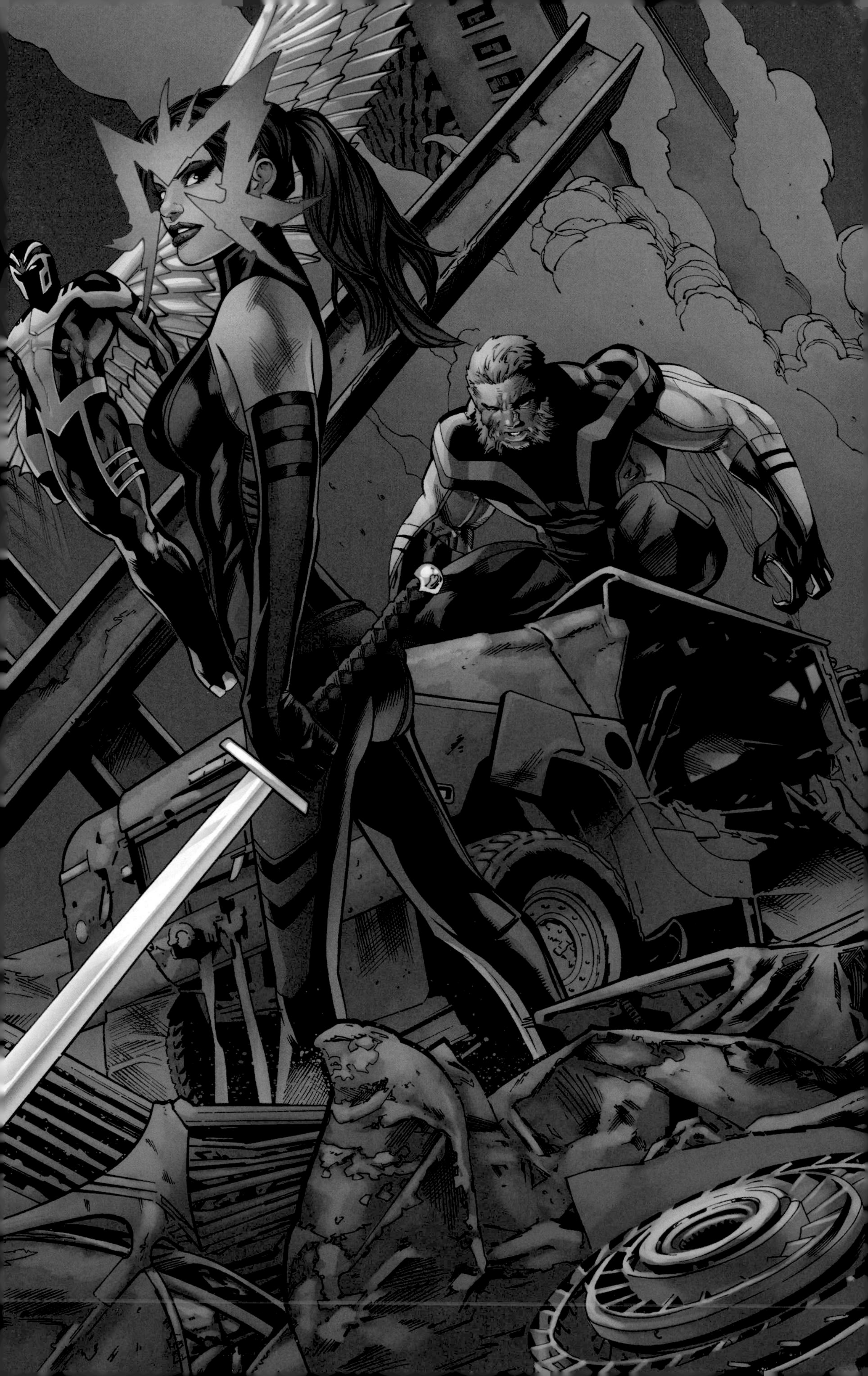

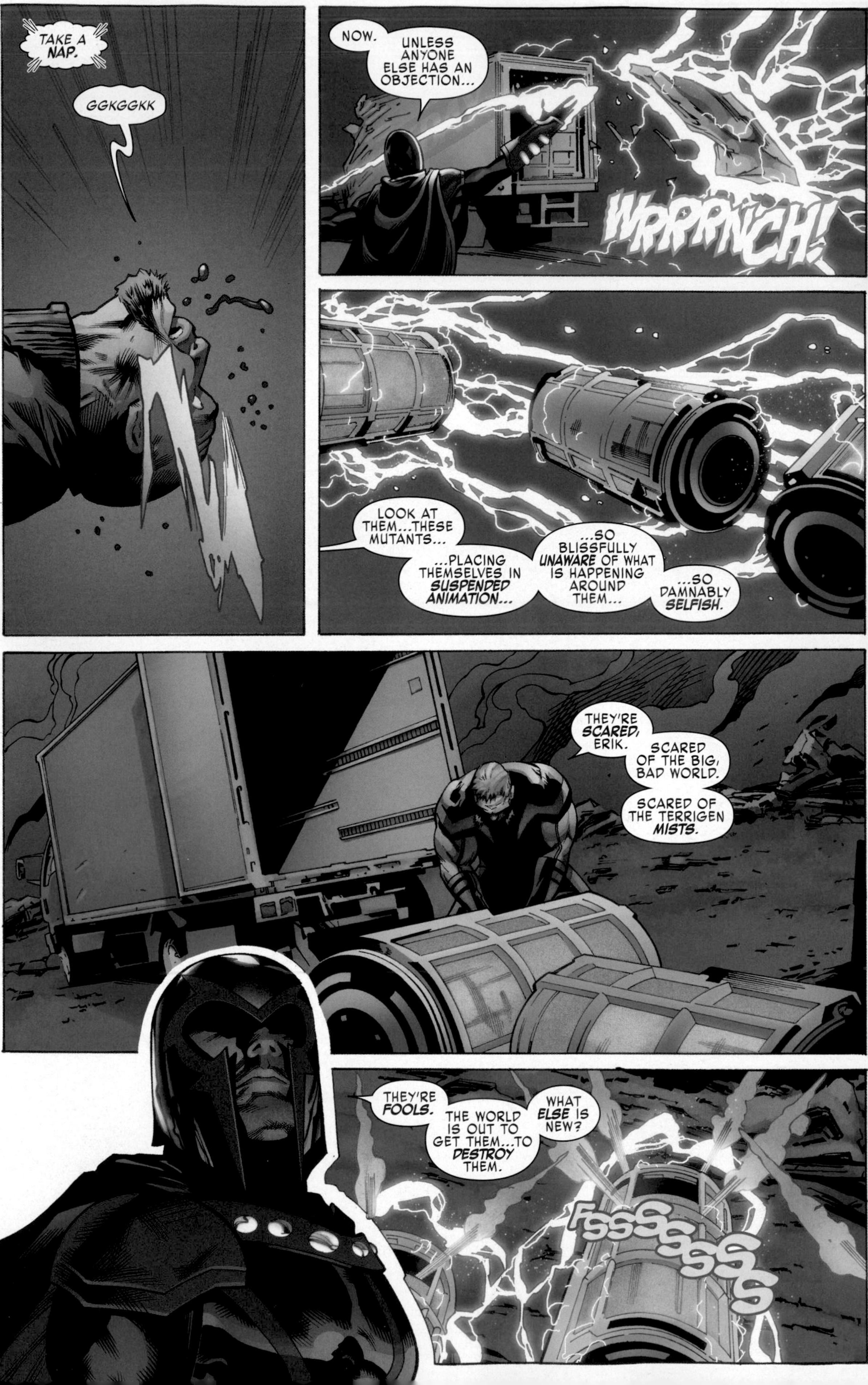
TAKE A NAP.
GGKGGKK
NOW.
UNLESS ANYONE ELSE HAS AN OBJECTION...
WRRRNCH!
LOOK AT THEM...THESE MUTANTS...
...PLACING THEMSELVES IN SUSPENDED ANIMATION...
...SO BLISSFULLY UNAWARE OF WHAT IS HAPPENING AROUND THEM...
...SO DAMNABLY SELFISH.
THEY'RE SCARED, ERIK.
SCARED OF THE BIG, BAD WORLD.
SCARED OF THE TERRIGEN MISTS.
THEY'RE FOOLS.
THE WORLD IS OUT TO GET THEM...TO DESTROY THEM.
WHAT ELSE IS NEW?
FSSSSSSSS

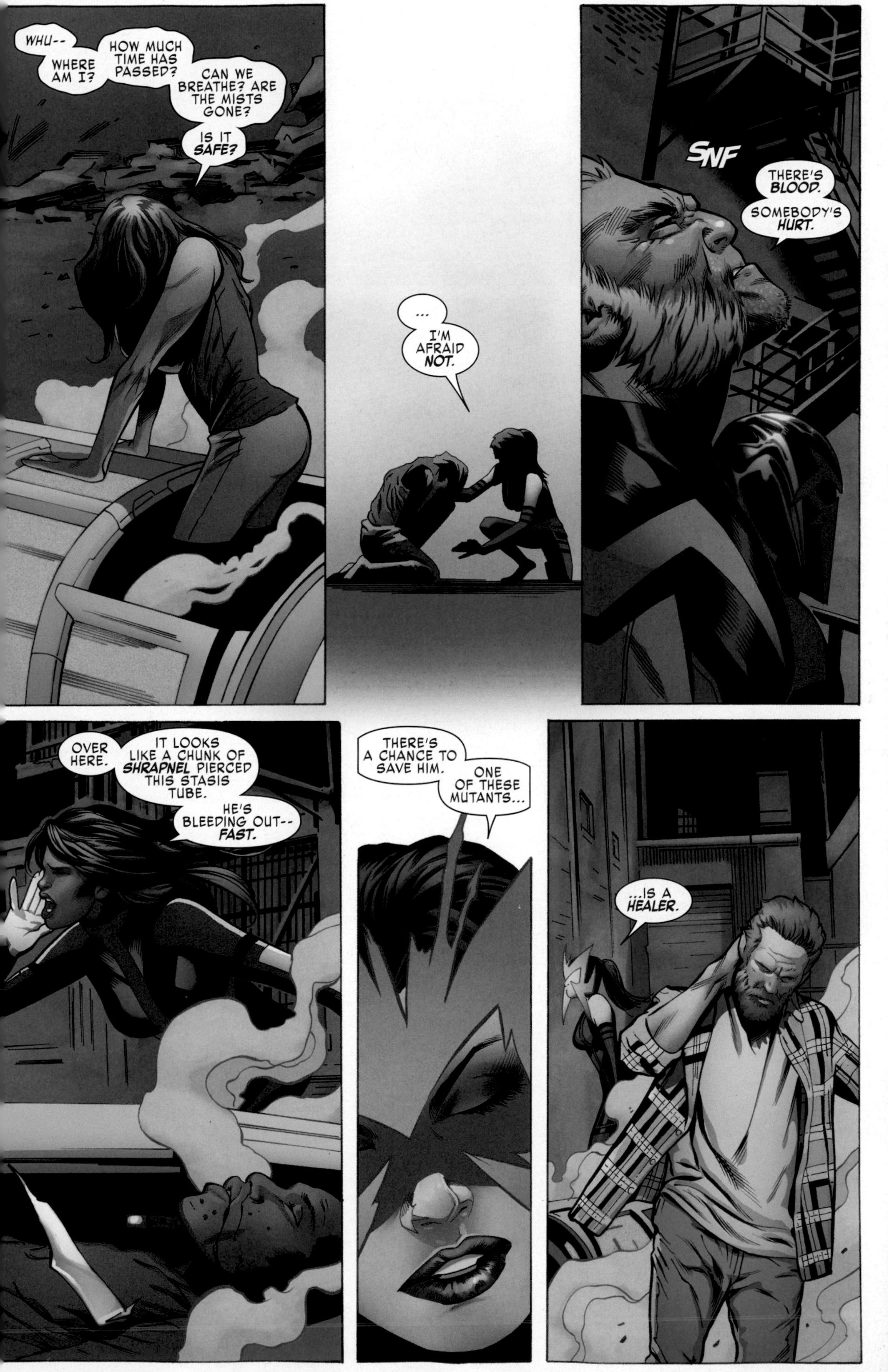
WHU--
WHERE AM I?
HOW MUCH TIME HAS PASSED?
CAN WE BREATHE? ARE THE MISTS GONE?
IS IT SAFE?
... I'M AFRAID NOT.
SNF
THERE'S BLOOD.
SOMEBODY'S HURT.
OVER HERE.
IT LOOKS LIKE A CHUNK OF SHRAPNEL PIERCED THIS STASIS TUBE.
HE'S BLEEDING OUT-- FAST.
THERE'S A CHANCE TO SAVE HIM.
ONE OF THESE MUTANTS...
...IS A HEALER.

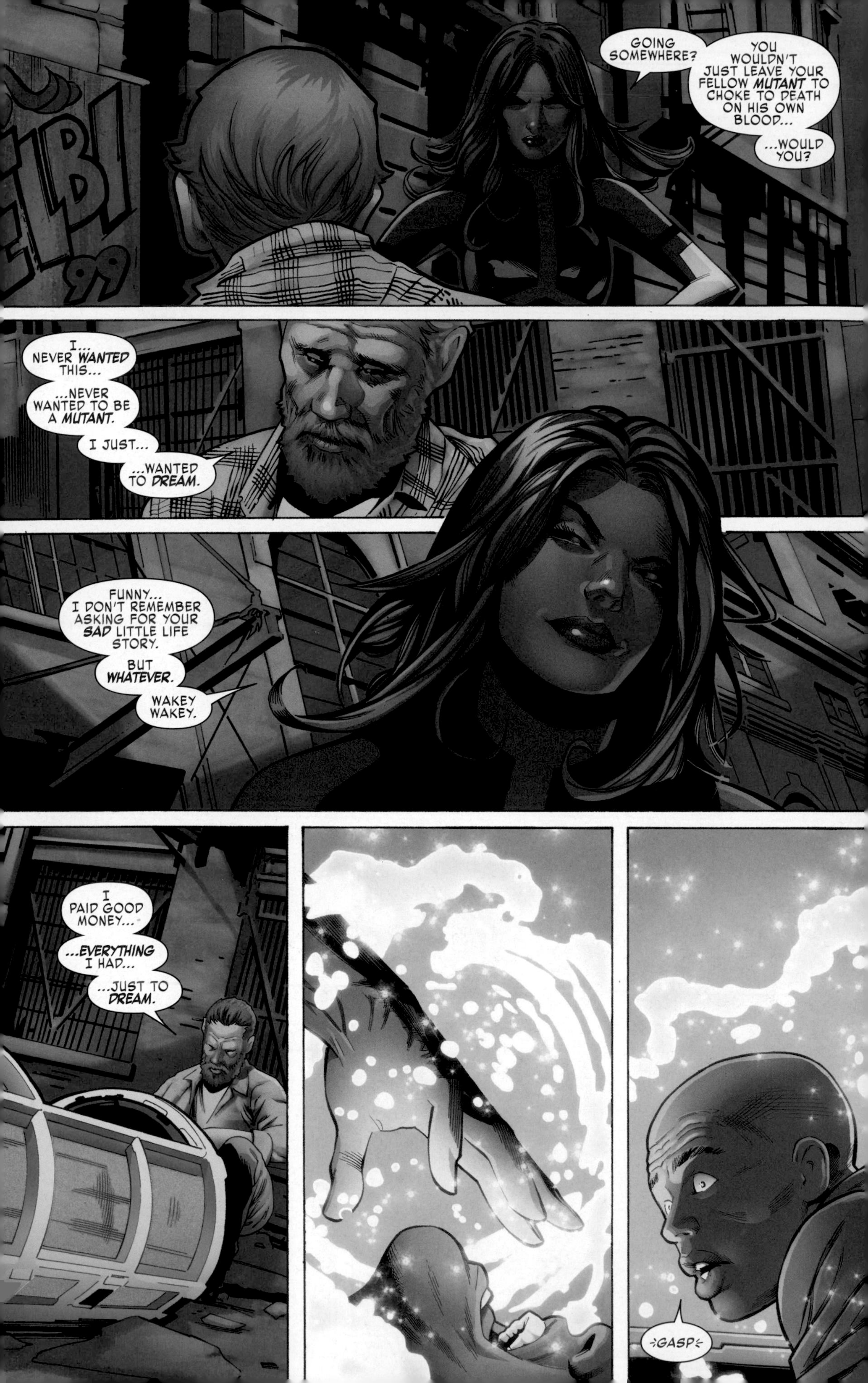
GOING SOMEWHERE?
YOU WOULDN'T JUST LEAVE YOUR FELLOW MUTANT TO CHOKE TO DEATH ON HIS OWN BLOOD...
...WOULD YOU?
I... NEVER WANTED THIS...
...NEVER WANTED TO BE A MUTANT.
I JUST...
...WANTED TO DREAM.
FUNNY... I DON'T REMEMBER ASKING FOR YOUR SAD LITTLE LIFE STORY.
BUT WHATEVER.
WAKEY WAKEY.
I PAID GOOD MONEY...
...EVERYTHING I HAD...
...JUST TO DREAM.
GASP

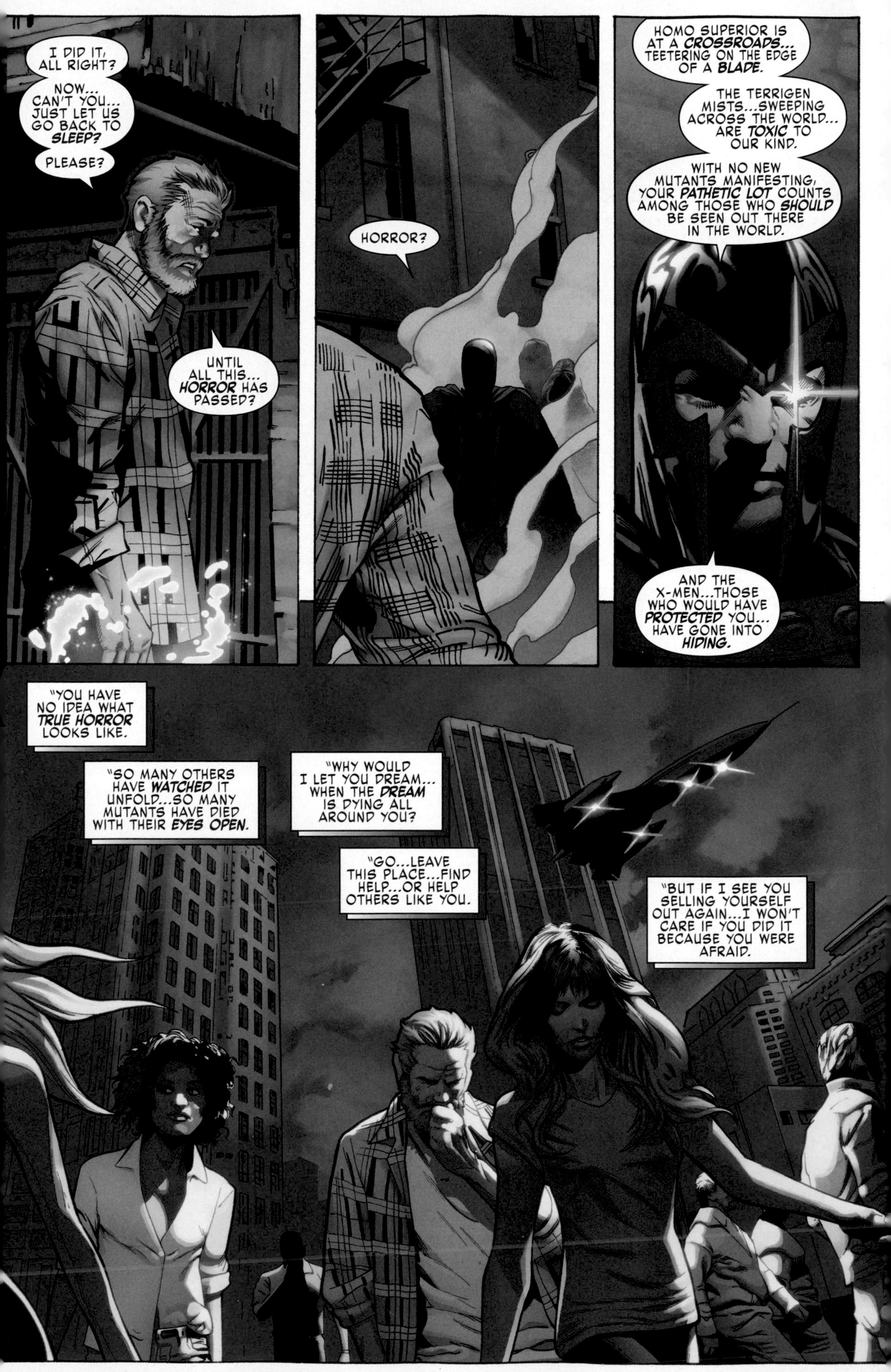
I DID IT, ALL RIGHT?
NOW... CAN'T YOU... JUST LET US GO BACK TO SLEEP?
PLEASE?
UNTIL ALL THIS... HORROR HAS PASSED?
HORROR?
HOMO SUPERIOR IS AT A CROSSROADS... TEETERING ON THE EDGE OF A BLADE.
THE TERRIGEN MISTS...SWEEPING ACROSS THE WORLD... ARE TOXIC TO OUR KIND.
WITH NO NEW MUTANTS MANIFESTING, YOUR PATHETIC LOT COUNTS AMONG THOSE WHO SHOULD BE SEEN OUT THERE IN THE WORLD.
AND THE X-MEN...THOSE WHO WOULD HAVE PROTECTED YOU... HAVE GONE INTO HIDING.
"YOU HAVE NO IDEA WHAT TRUE HORROR LOOKS LIKE.
"SO MANY OTHERS HAVE WATCHED IT UNFOLD...SO MANY MUTANTS HAVE DIED WITH THEIR EYES OPEN.
"WHY WOULD I LET YOU DREAM... WHEN THE DREAM IS DYING ALL AROUND YOU?
"GO...LEAVE THIS PLACE...FIND HELP...OR HELP OTHERS LIKE YOU.
"BUT IF I SEE YOU SELLING YOURSELF OUT AGAIN...I WON'T CARE IF YOU DID IT BECAUSE YOU WERE AFRAID.

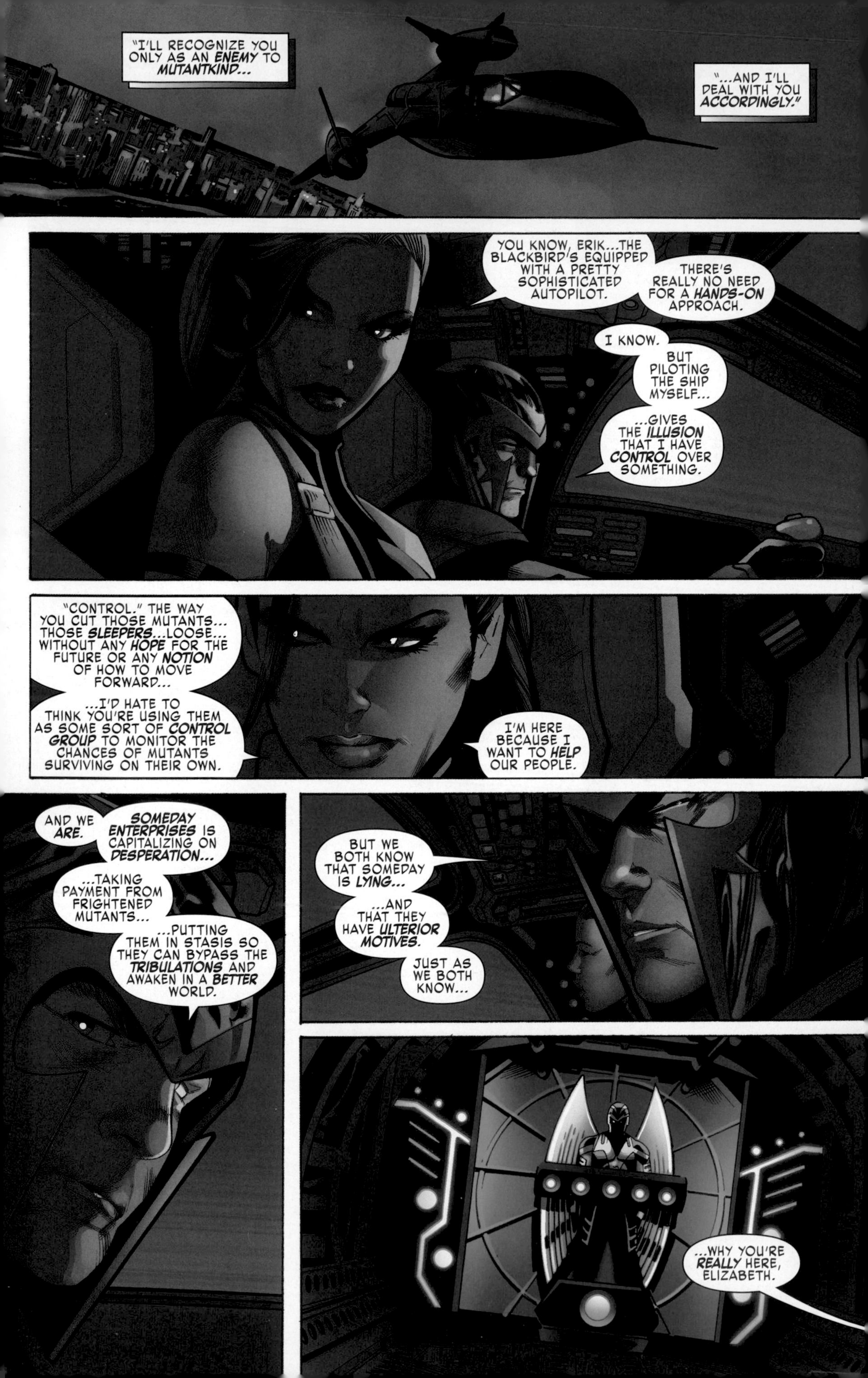
"I'LL RECOGNIZE YOU ONLY AS AN ENEMY TO MUTANTKIND...
"...AND I'LL DEAL WITH YOU ACCORDINGLY."
YOU KNOW, ERIK...THE BLACKBIRD'S EQUIPPED WITH A PRETTY SOPHISTICATED AUTOPILOT.
THERE'S REALLY NO NEED FOR A HANDS-ON APPROACH.
I KNOW.
BUT PILOTING THE SHIP MYSELF...
...GIVES THE ILLUSION THAT I HAVE CONTROL OVER SOMETHING.
"CONTROL." THE WAY YOU CUT THOSE MUTANTS... THOSE SLEEPERS...LOOSE... WITHOUT ANY HOPE FOR THE FUTURE OR ANY NOTION OF HOW TO MOVE FORWARD...
...I'D HATE TO THINK YOU'RE USING THEM AS SOME SORT OF CONTROL GROUP TO MONITOR THE CHANCES OF MUTANTS SURVIVING ON THEIR OWN.
I'M HERE BECAUSE I WANT TO HELP OUR PEOPLE.
AND WE ARE.
SOMEDAY ENTERPRISES IS CAPITALIZING ON DESPERATION...
...TAKING PAYMENT FROM FRIGHTENED MUTANTS...
...PUTTING THEM IN STASIS SO THEY CAN BYPASS THE TRIBULATIONS AND AWAKEN IN A BETTER WORLD.
BUT WE BOTH KNOW THAT SOMEDAY IS LYING...
...AND THAT THEY HAVE ULTERIOR MOTIVES.
JUST AS WE BOTH KNOW...
...WHY YOU'RE REALLY HERE, ELIZABETH.

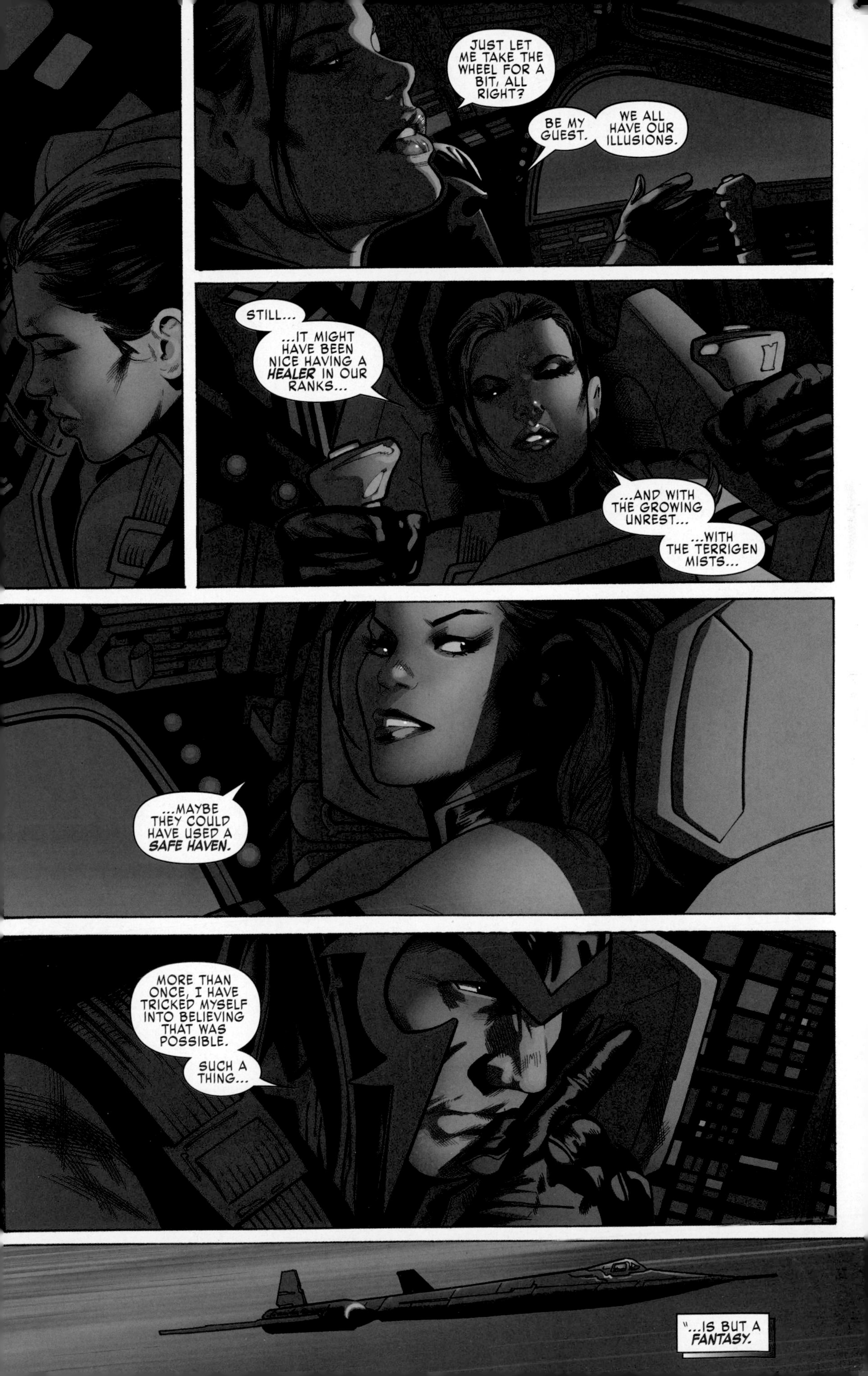
JUST LET ME TAKE THE WHEEL FOR A BIT, ALL RIGHT?
BE MY GUEST.
WE ALL HAVE OUR ILLUSIONS.
STILL...
...IT MIGHT HAVE BEEN NICE HAVING A HEALER IN OUR RANKS...
...AND WITH THE GROWING UNREST...
...WITH THE TERRIGEN MISTS...
...MAYBE THEY COULD HAVE USED A SAFE HAVEN.
MORE THAN ONCE, I HAVE TRICKED MYSELF INTO BELIEVING THAT WAS POSSIBLE.
SUCH A THING...
"...IS BUT A FANTASY.

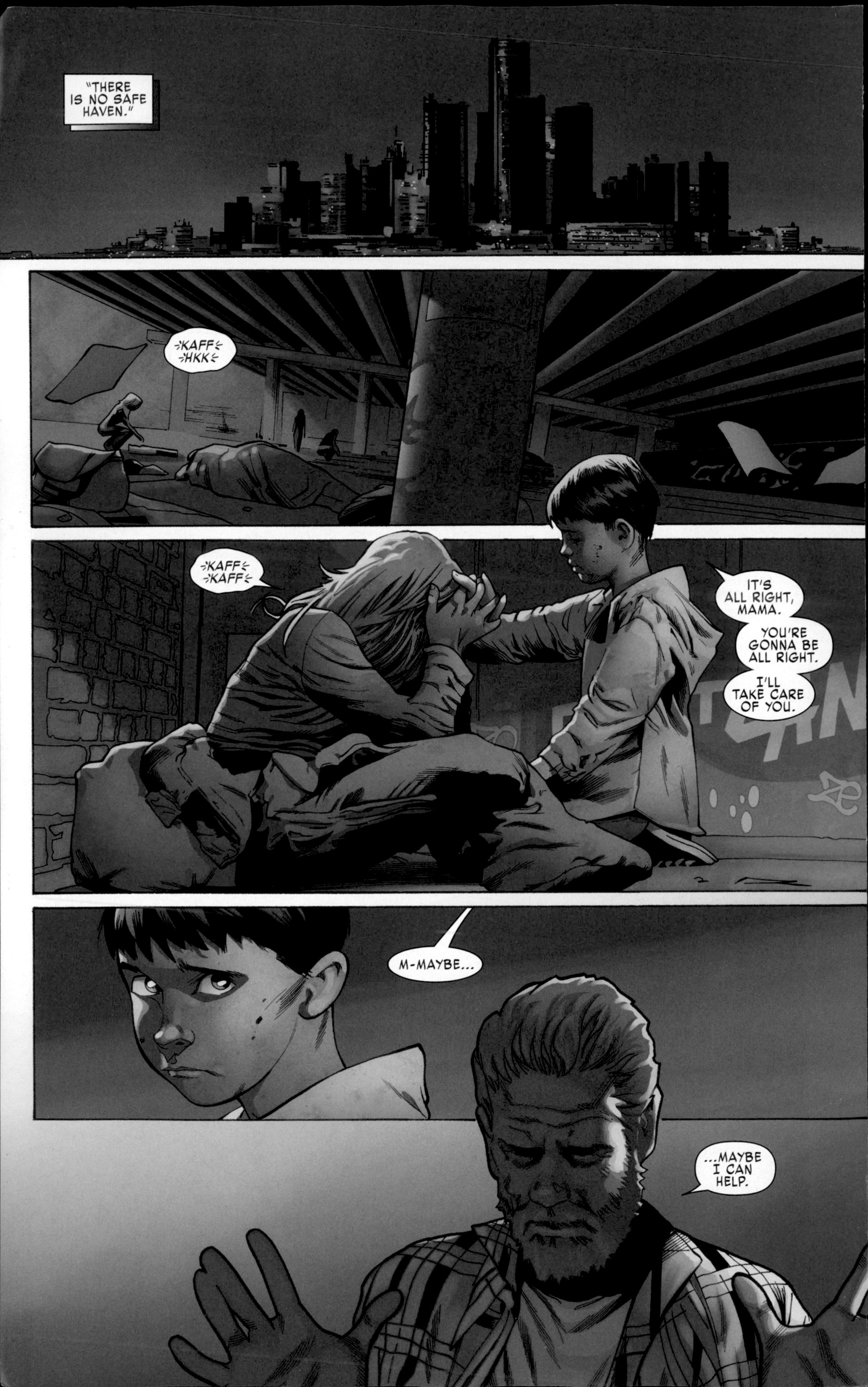
"THERE IS NO SAFE HAVEN."
KAFF HKK
KAFF KAFF
IT'S ALL RIGHT, MAMA.
YOU'RE GONNA BE ALL RIGHT.
I'LL TAKE CARE OF YOU.
M-MAYBE...
...MAYBE I CAN HELP.

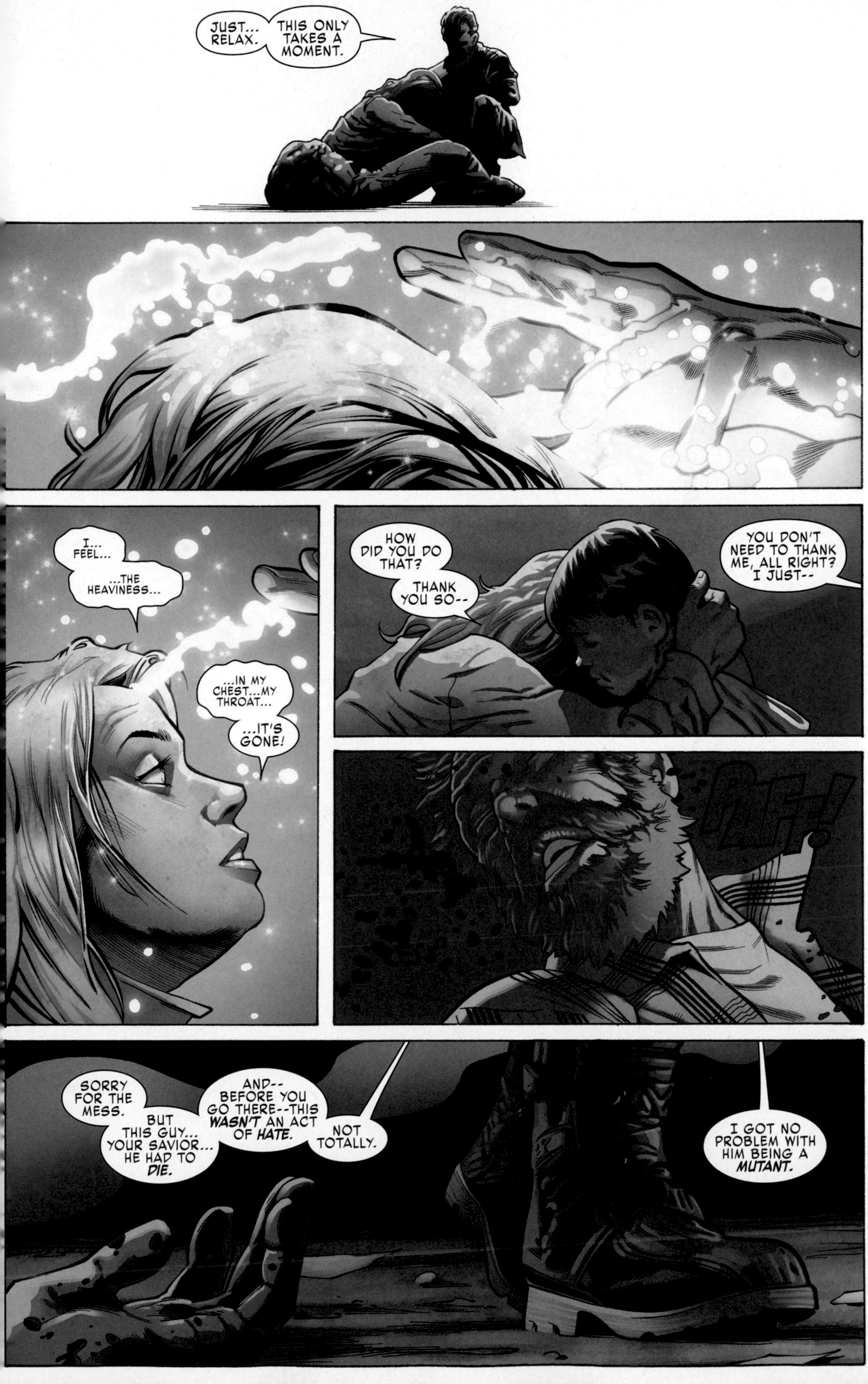
JUST... RELAX.
THIS ONLY TAKES A MOMENT.
I... FEEL...
...THE HEAVINESS...
...IN MY CHEST...MY THROAT...
...IT'S GONE!
HOW DID YOU DO THAT?
THANK YOU SO--
YOU DON'T NEED TO THANK ME, ALL RIGHT? I JUST--
SORRY FOR THE MESS.
BUT THIS GUY... YOUR SAVIOR... HE HAD TO DIE.
AND--BEFORE YOU GO THERE--THIS WASN'T AN ACT OF HATE.
NOT TOTALLY.
I GOT NO PROBLEM WITH HIM BEING A MUTANT.

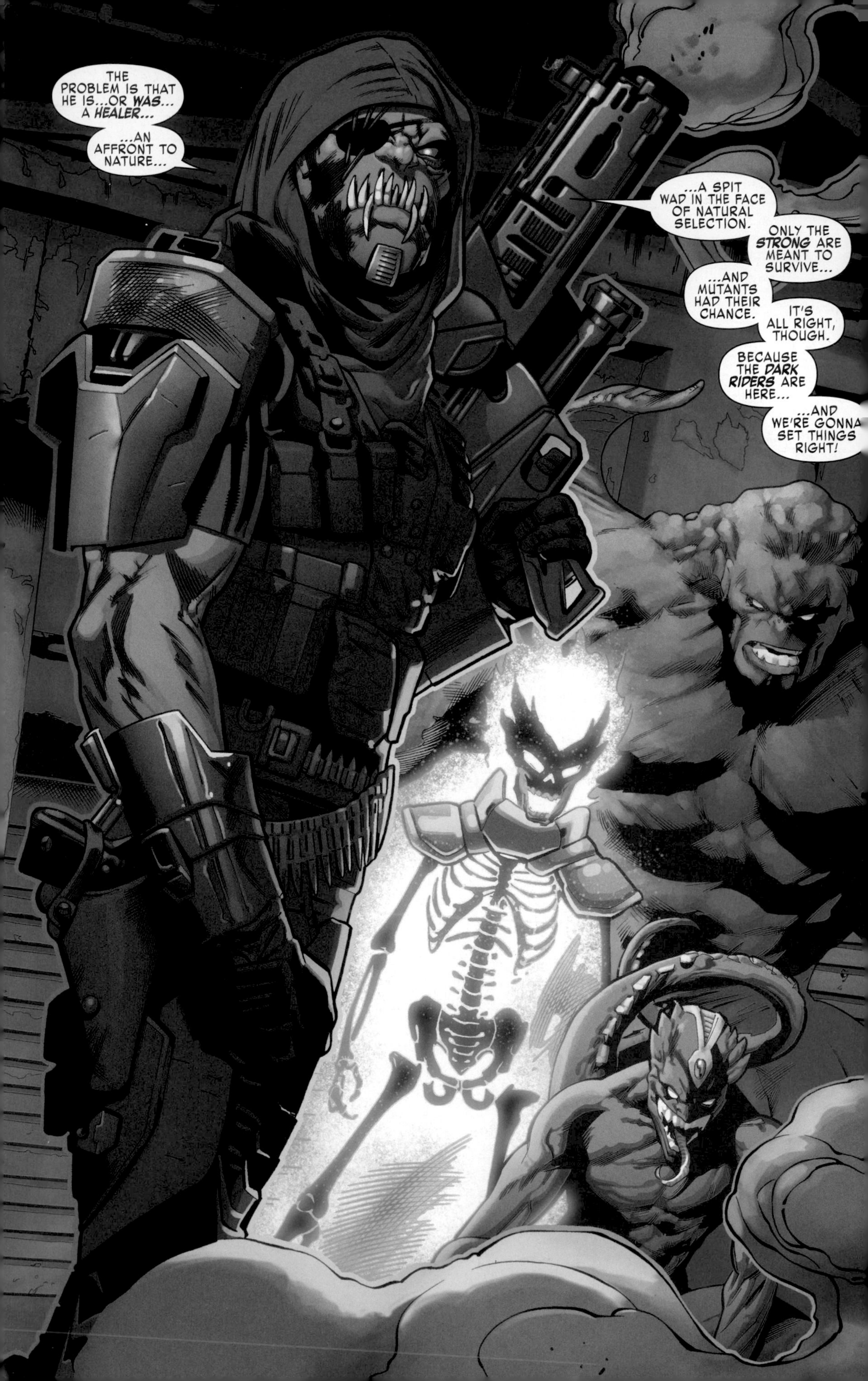
THE PROBLEM IS THAT HE IS...OR WAS... A HEALER...
...AN AFFRONT TO NATURE...
...A SPIT WAD IN THE FACE OF NATURAL SELECTION.
ONLY THE STRONG ARE MEANT TO SURVIVE...
...AND MUTANTS HAD THEIR CHANCE.
IT'S ALL RIGHT, THOUGH.
BECAUSE THE DARK RIDERS ARE HERE...
...AND WE'RE GONNA SET THINGS RIGHT!

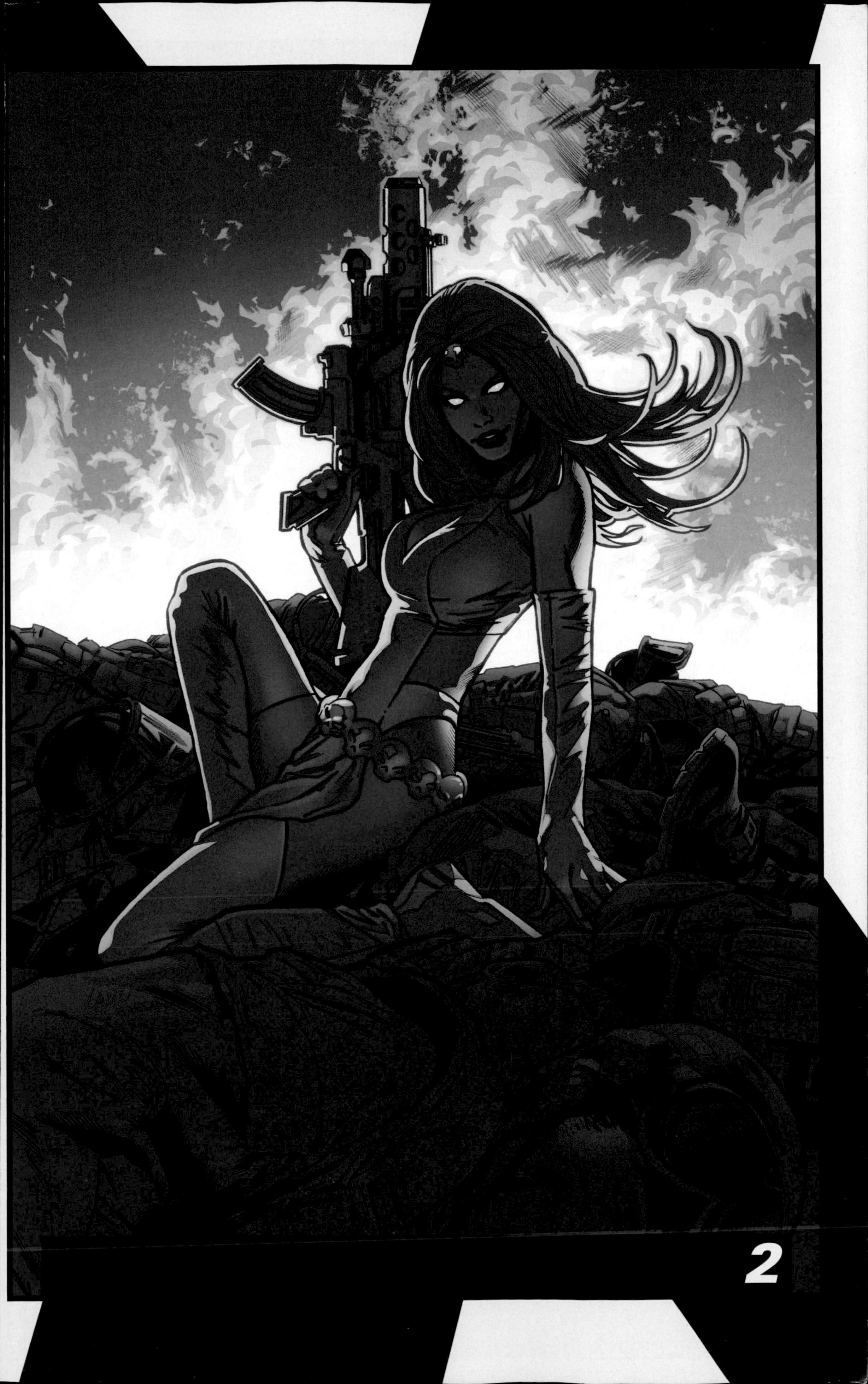
2

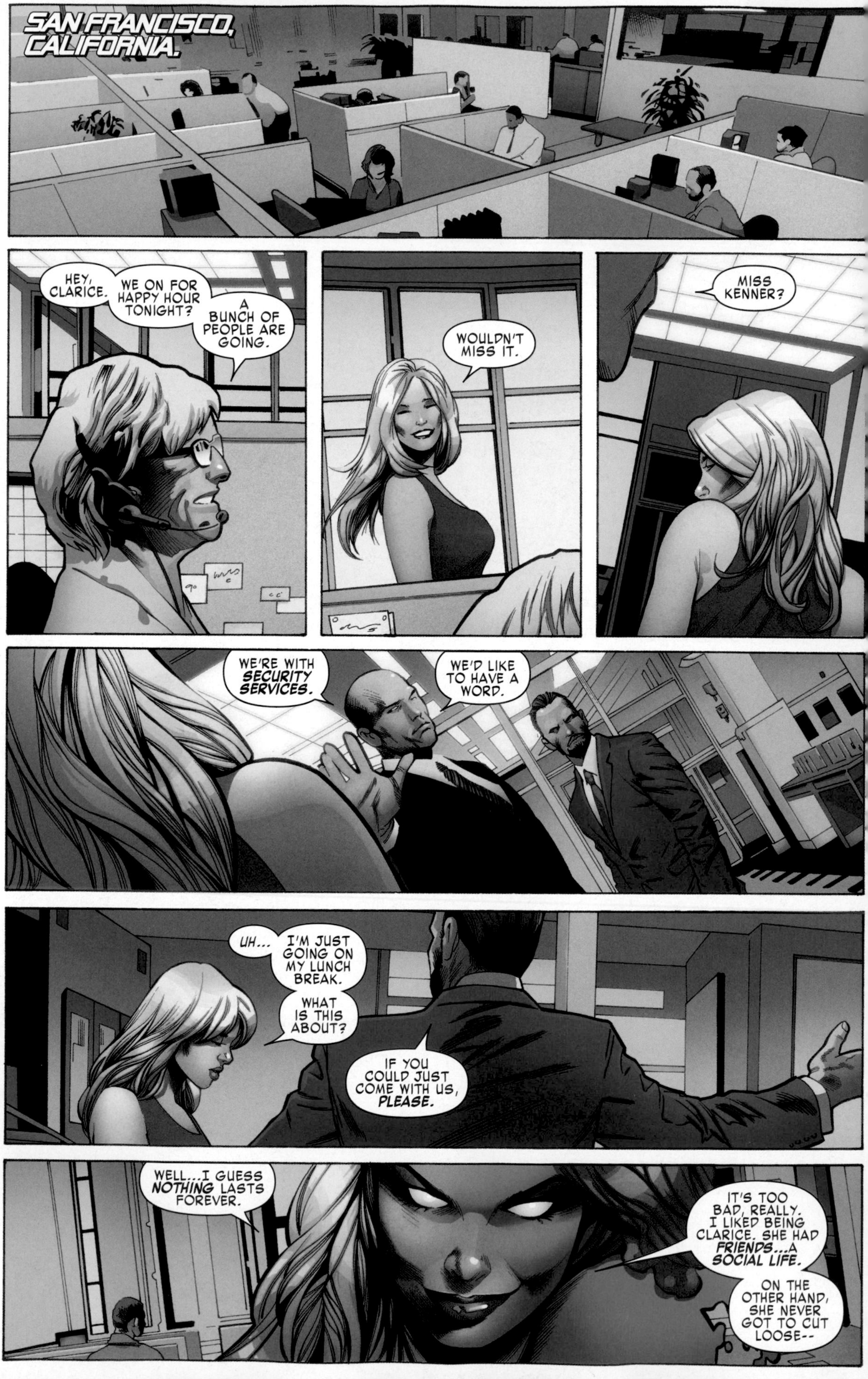
SAN FRANCISCO, CALIFORNIA.
HEY, CLARICE.
WE ON FOR HAPPY HOUR TONIGHT?
A BUNCH OF PEOPLE ARE GOING.
WOULDN'T MISS IT.
MISS KENNER?
WE'RE WITH SECURITY SERVICES.
WE'D LIKE TO HAVE A WORD.
UH...
I'M JUST GOING ON MY LUNCH BREAK.
WHAT IS THIS ABOUT?
IF YOU COULD JUST COME WITH US, PLEASE.
WELL...I GUESS NOTHING LASTS FOREVER.
IT'S TOO BAD, REALLY. I LIKED BEING CLARICE. SHE HAD FRIENDS...A SOCIAL LIFE.
ON THE OTHER HAND, SHE NEVER GOT TO CUT LOOSE--

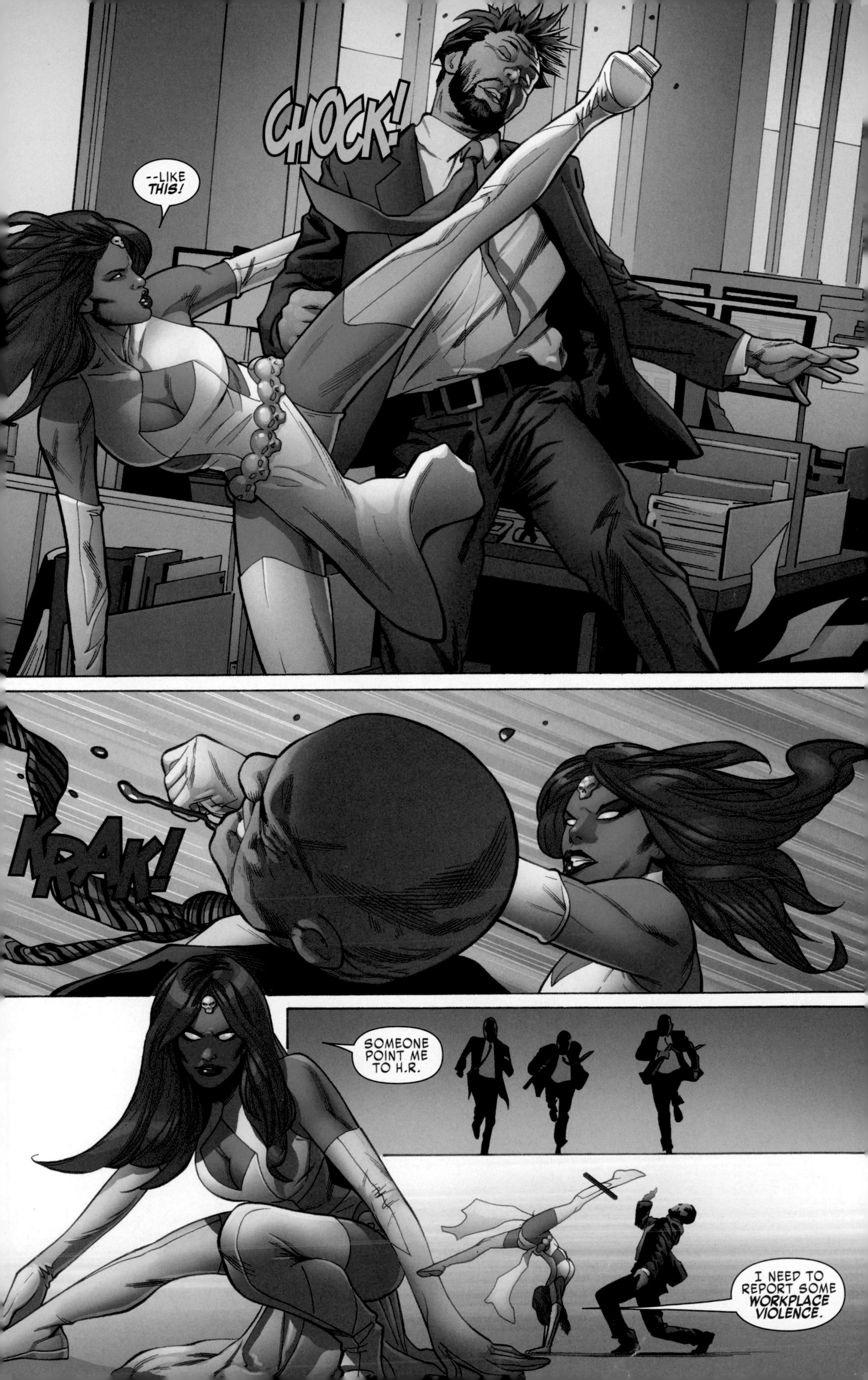
CHOCK!
--LIKE THIS!
KRAK!
SOMEONE POINT ME TO H.R.
I NEED TO REPORT SOME WORKPLACE VIOLENCE.

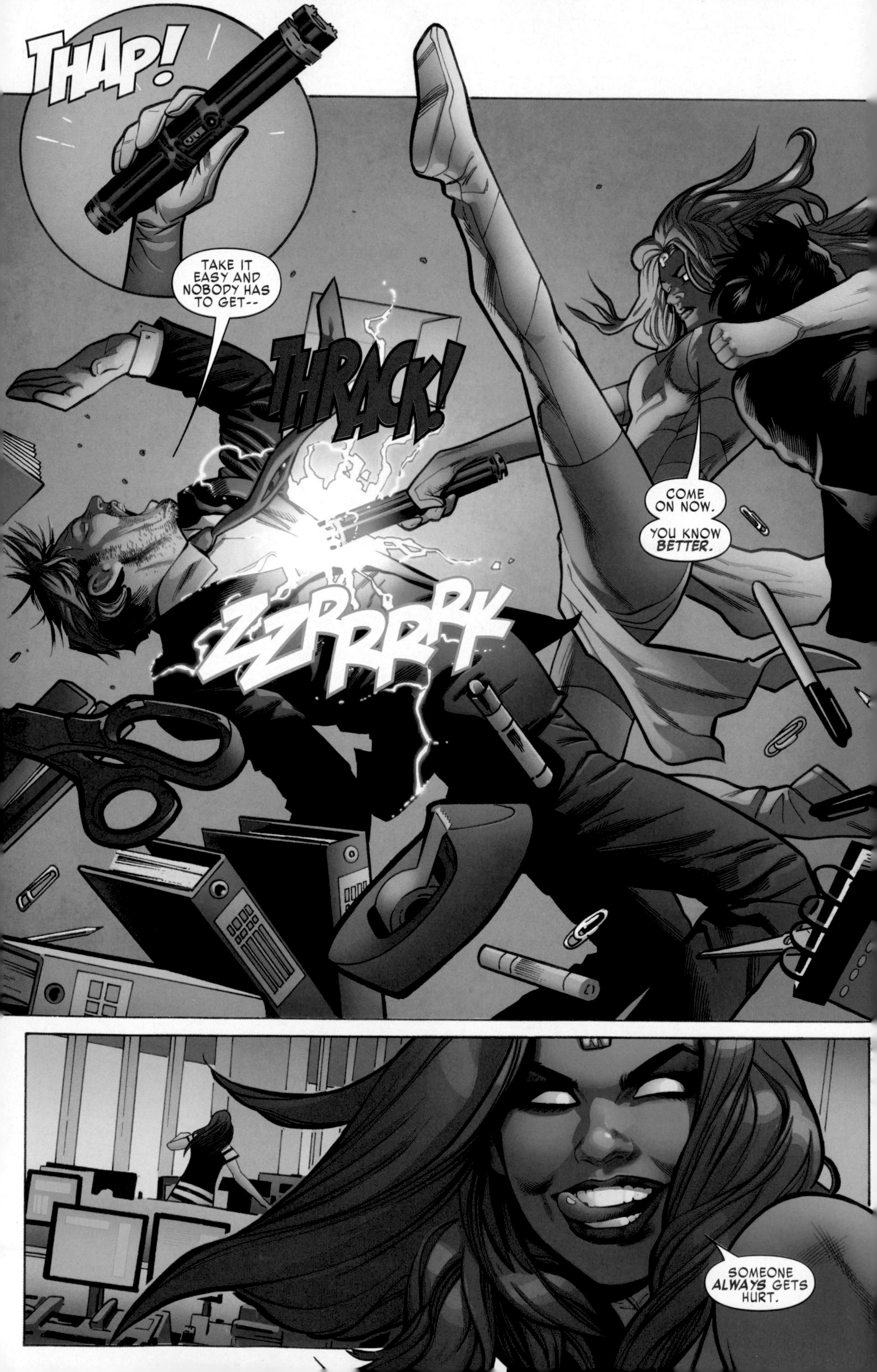
THAP!
TAKE IT EASY AND NOBODY HAS TO GET--
THRACK!
ZZRRRRK
COME ON NOW.
YOU KNOW BETTER.
SOMEONE ALWAYS GETS HURT.

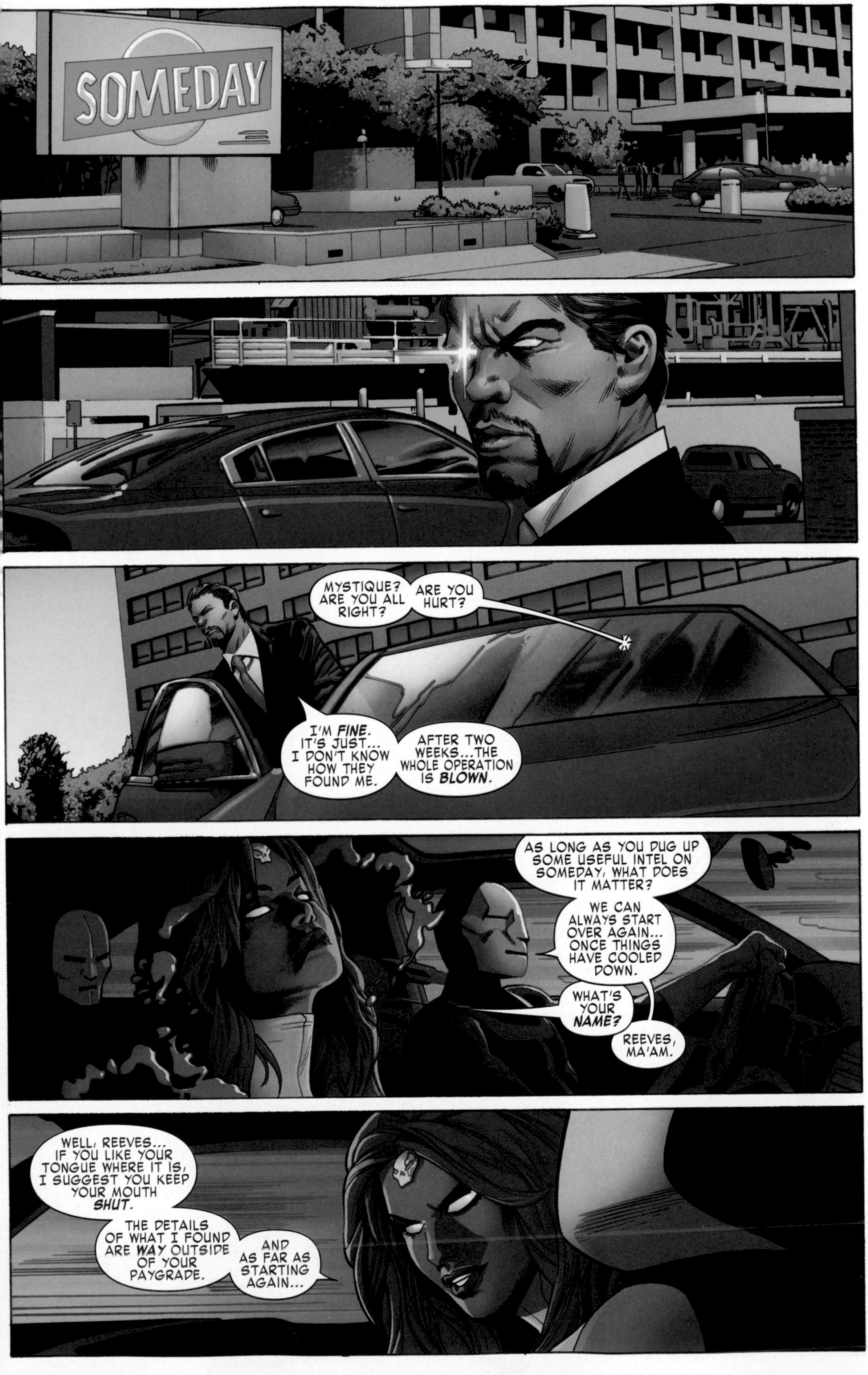
SOMEDAY
MYSTIQUE? ARE YOU ALL RIGHT?
ARE YOU HURT?
I'M **FINE**. IT'S JUST... I DON'T KNOW HOW THEY FOUND ME.
AFTER TWO WEEKS...THE WHOLE OPERATION IS **BLOWN**.
AS LONG AS YOU DUG UP SOME USEFUL INTEL ON SOMEDAY, WHAT DOES IT MATTER?
WE CAN ALWAYS START OVER AGAIN... ONCE THINGS HAVE COOLED DOWN.
WHAT'S YOUR **NAME?**
REEVES, MA'AM.
WELL, REEVES... IF YOU LIKE YOUR TONGUE WHERE IT IS, I SUGGEST YOU KEEP YOUR MOUTH **SHUT**.
THE DETAILS OF WHAT I FOUND ARE **WAY** OUTSIDE OF YOUR PAYGRADE.
AND AS FAR AS STARTING AGAIN...

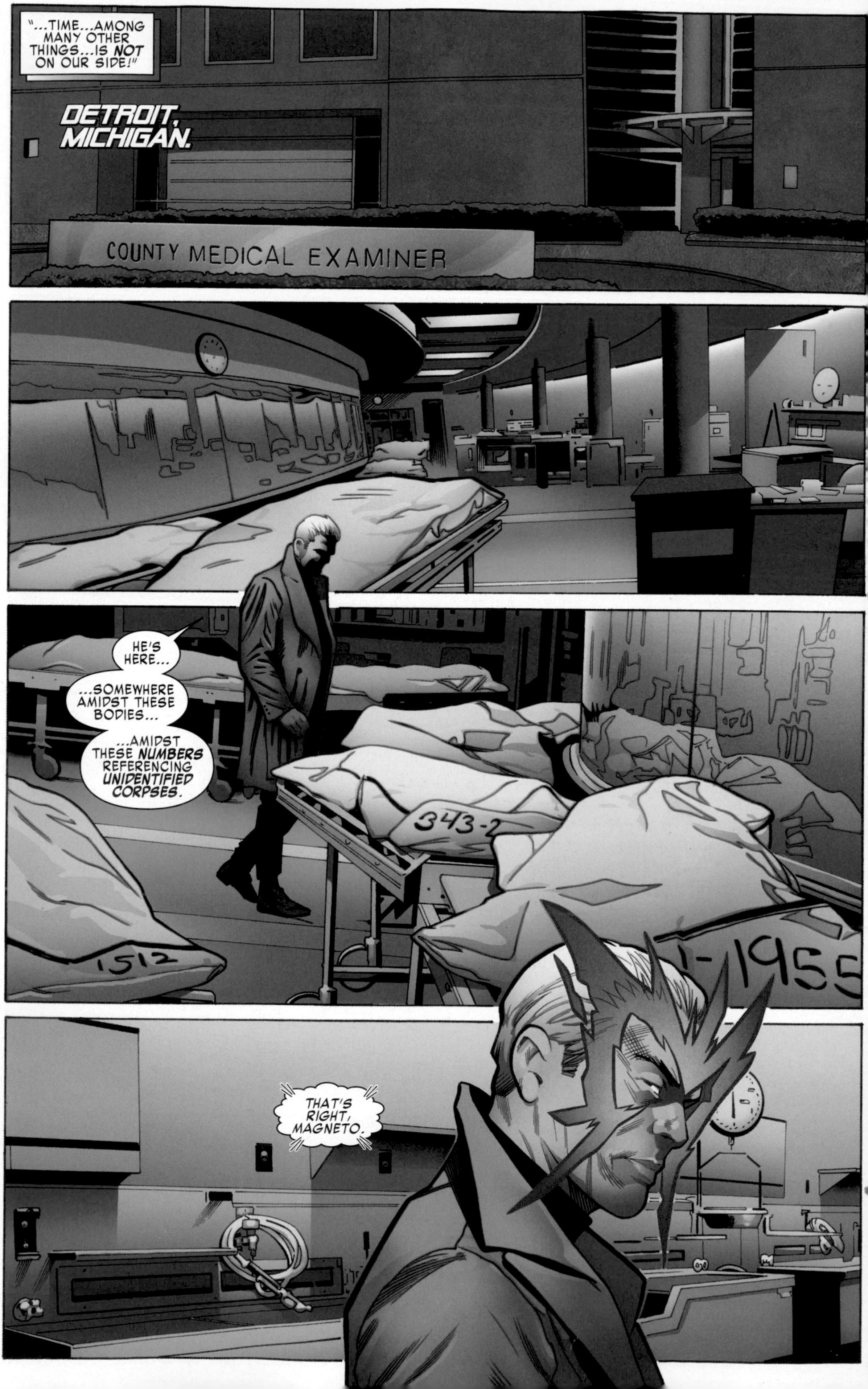
"...TIME...AMONG MANY OTHER THINGS...IS NOT ON OUR SIDE!"
DETROIT, MICHIGAN.
COUNTY MEDICAL EXAMINER
HE'S HERE...
...SOMEWHERE AMIDST THESE BODIES...
...AMIDST THESE NUMBERS REFERENCING UNIDENTIFIED CORPSES.
343-2
1512
1-1955
THAT'S RIGHT, MAGNETO.

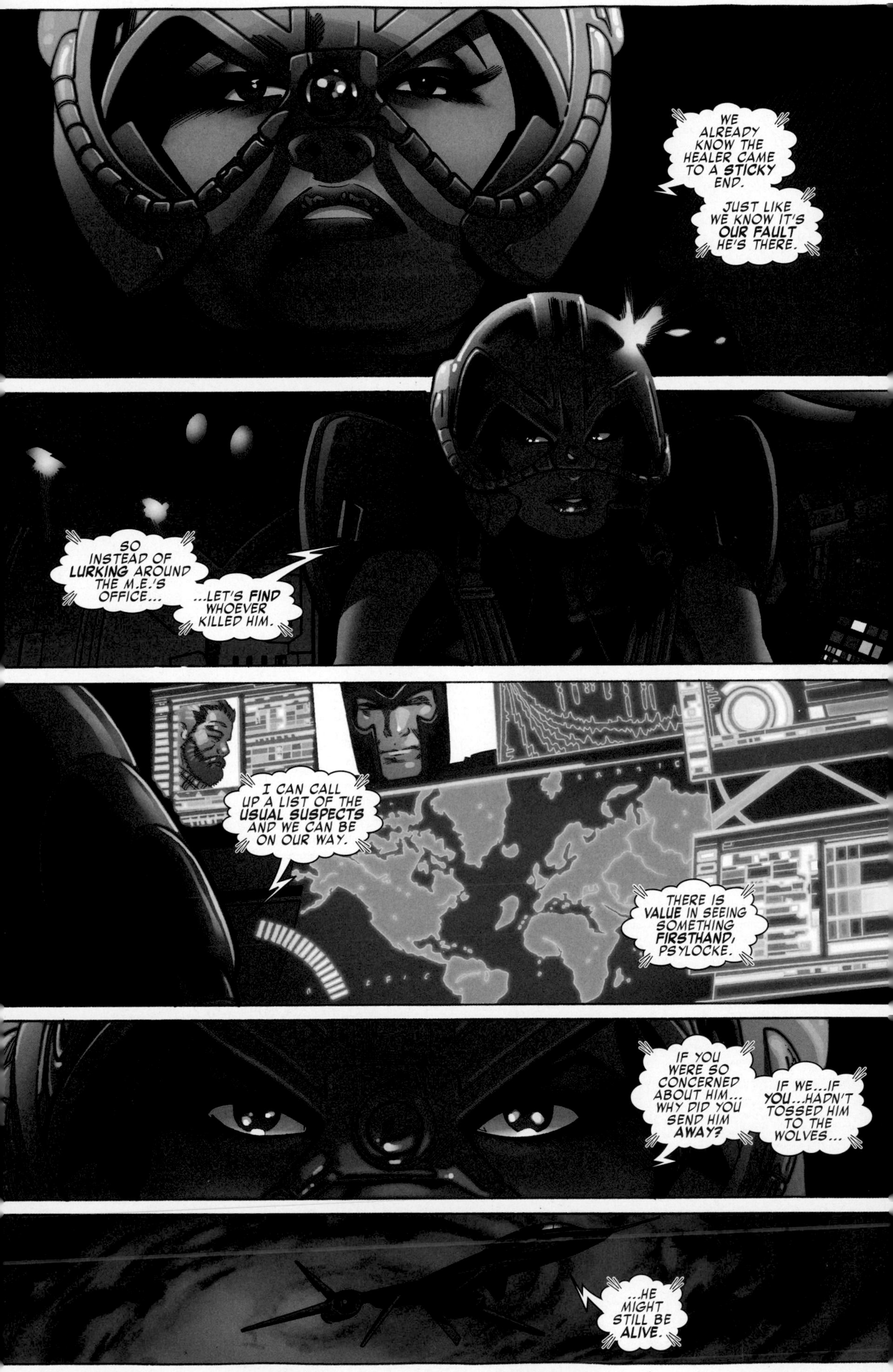
WE ALREADY KNOW THE HEALER CAME TO A STICKY END.
JUST LIKE WE KNOW IT'S OUR FAULT HE'S THERE.
SO INSTEAD OF LURKING AROUND THE M.E.'S OFFICE...
...LET'S FIND WHOEVER KILLED HIM.
I CAN CALL UP A LIST OF THE USUAL SUSPECTS AND WE CAN BE ON OUR WAY.
THERE IS VALUE IN SEEING SOMETHING FIRSTHAND, PSYLOCKE.
IF YOU WERE SO CONCERNED ABOUT HIM... WHY DID YOU SEND HIM AWAY?
IF WE...IF YOU...HADN'T TOSSED HIM TO THE WOLVES...
...HE MIGHT STILL BE ALIVE.

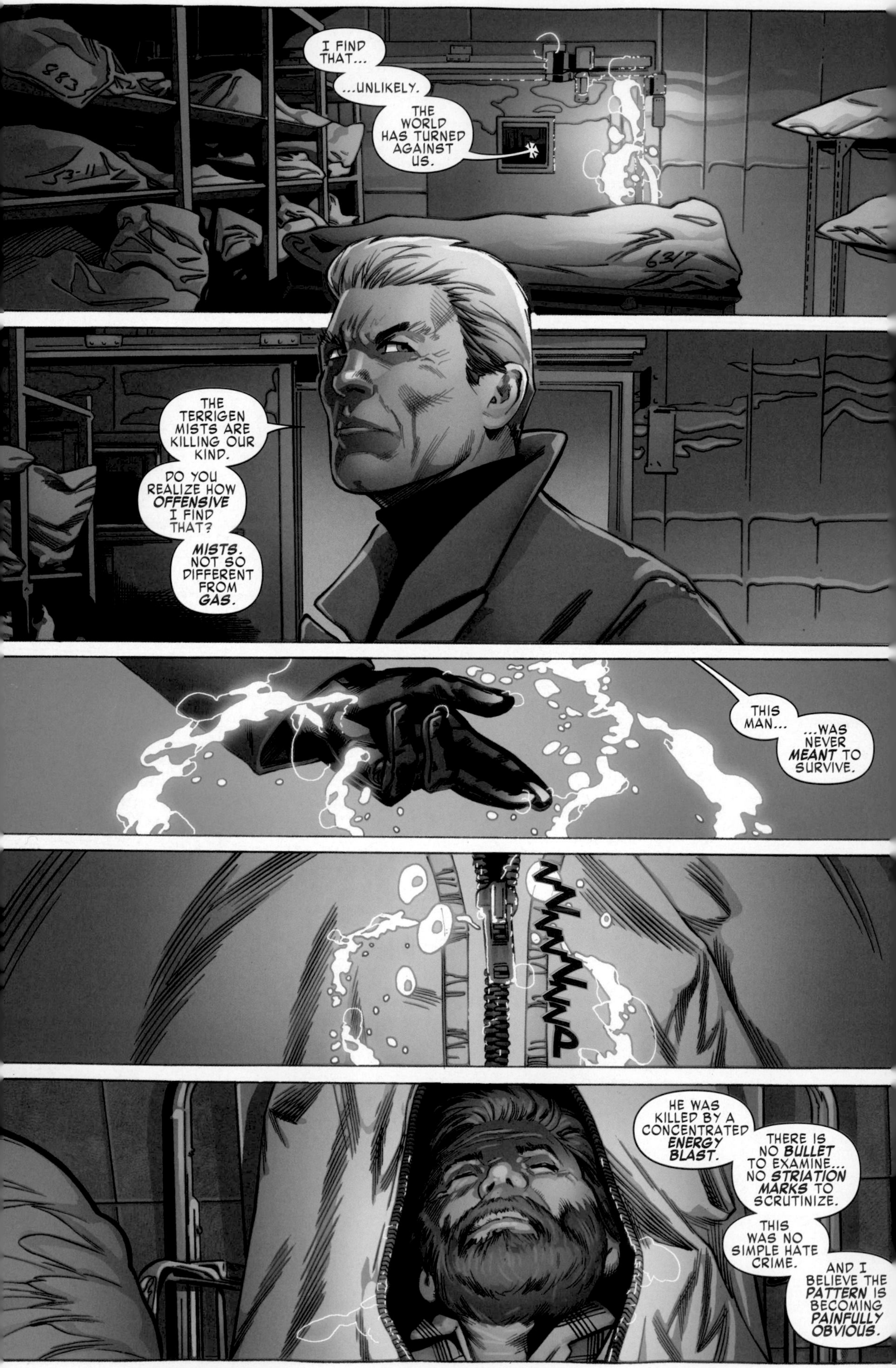
I FIND THAT...
...UNLIKELY.
THE WORLD HAS TURNED AGAINST US.
THE TERRIGEN MISTS ARE KILLING OUR KIND.
DO YOU REALIZE HOW OFFENSIVE I FIND THAT?
MISTS. NOT SO DIFFERENT FROM GAS.
THIS MAN...
...WAS NEVER MEANT TO SURVIVE.
VVVWWWWP
HE WAS KILLED BY A CONCENTRATED ENERGY BLAST.
THERE IS NO BULLET TO EXAMINE... NO STRIATION MARKS TO SCRUTINIZE.
THIS WAS NO SIMPLE HATE CRIME.
AND I BELIEVE THE PATTERN IS BECOMING PAINFULLY OBVIOUS.

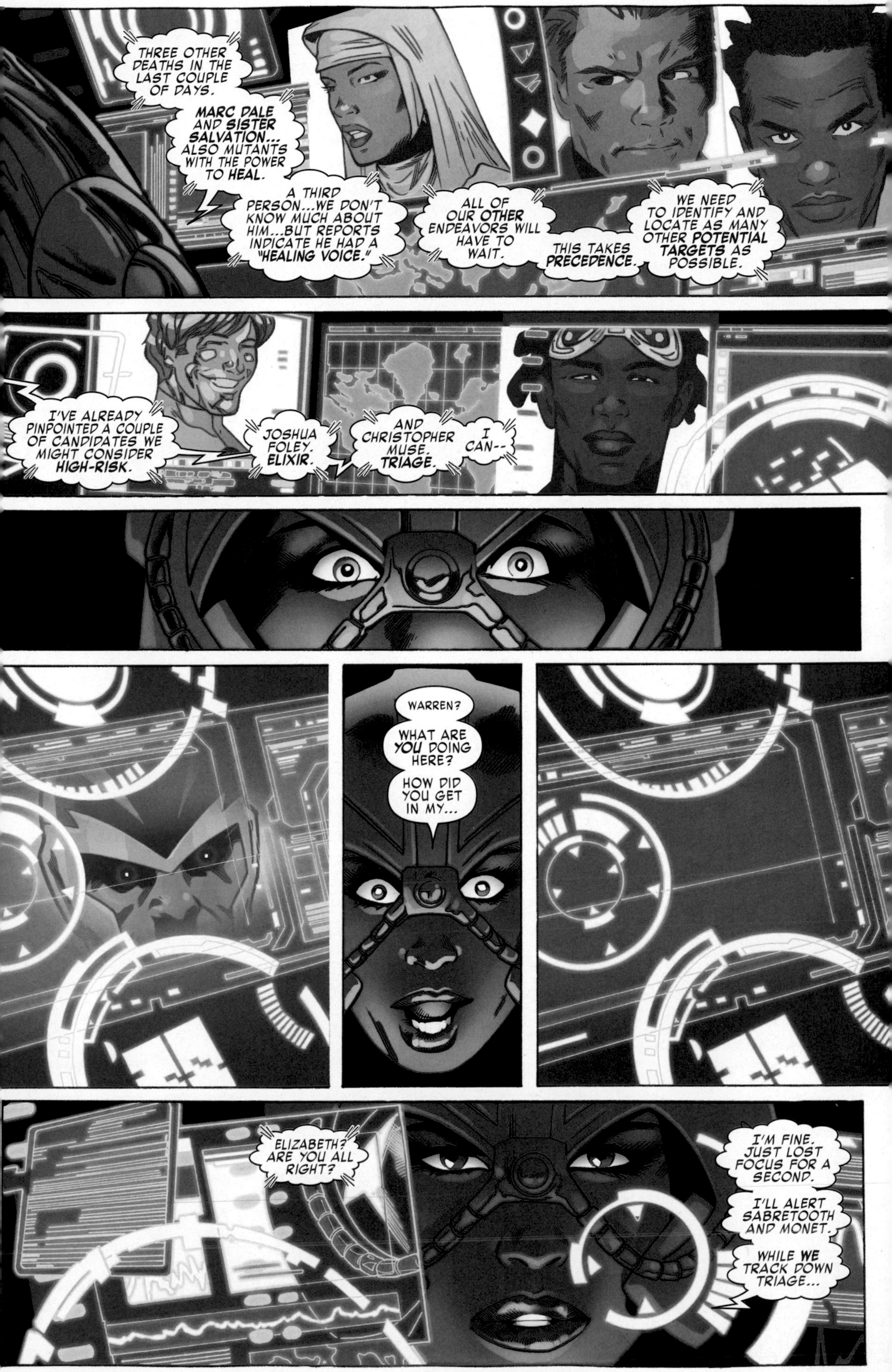
THREE OTHER DEATHS IN THE LAST COUPLE OF DAYS.
MARC DALE AND SISTER SALVATION... ALSO MUTANTS WITH THE POWER TO HEAL.
A THIRD PERSON...WE DON'T KNOW MUCH ABOUT HIM...BUT REPORTS INDICATE HE HAD A "HEALING VOICE."
ALL OF OUR OTHER ENDEAVORS WILL HAVE TO WAIT.
THIS TAKES PRECEDENCE.
WE NEED TO IDENTIFY AND LOCATE AS MANY OTHER POTENTIAL TARGETS AS POSSIBLE.
I'VE ALREADY PINPOINTED A COUPLE OF CANDIDATES WE MIGHT CONSIDER HIGH-RISK.
JOSHUA FOLEY. ELIXIR.
AND CHRISTOPHER MUSE. TRIAGE.
I CAN--
WARREN?
WHAT ARE YOU DOING HERE?
HOW DID YOU GET IN MY...
ELIZABETH? ARE YOU ALL RIGHT?
I'M FINE. JUST LOST FOCUS FOR A SECOND.
I'LL ALERT SABRETOOTH AND MONET.
WHILE WE TRACK DOWN TRIAGE...

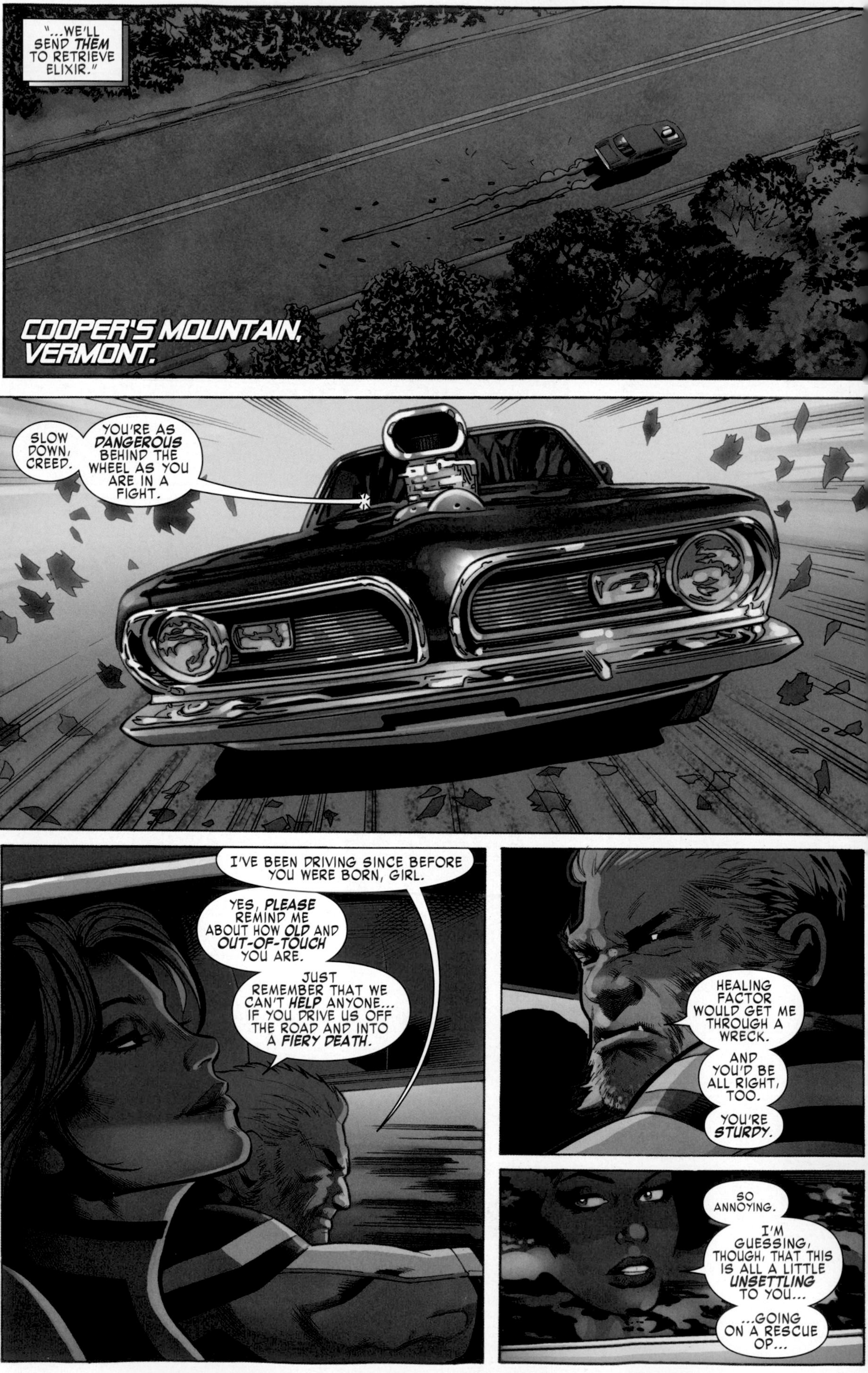
"...WE'LL SEND THEM TO RETRIEVE ELIXIR."
COOPER'S MOUNTAIN, VERMONT.
SLOW DOWN, CREED.
YOU'RE AS DANGEROUS BEHIND THE WHEEL AS YOU ARE IN A FIGHT.
I'VE BEEN DRIVING SINCE BEFORE YOU WERE BORN, GIRL.
YES, PLEASE REMIND ME ABOUT HOW OLD AND OUT-OF-TOUCH YOU ARE.
JUST REMEMBER THAT WE CAN'T HELP ANYONE... IF YOU DRIVE US OFF THE ROAD AND INTO A FIERY DEATH.
HEALING FACTOR WOULD GET ME THROUGH A WRECK.
AND YOU'D BE ALL RIGHT, TOO.
YOU'RE STURDY.
SO ANNOYING.
I'M GUESSING, THOUGH, THAT THIS IS ALL A LITTLE UNSETTLING TO YOU...
...GOING ON A RESCUE OP...

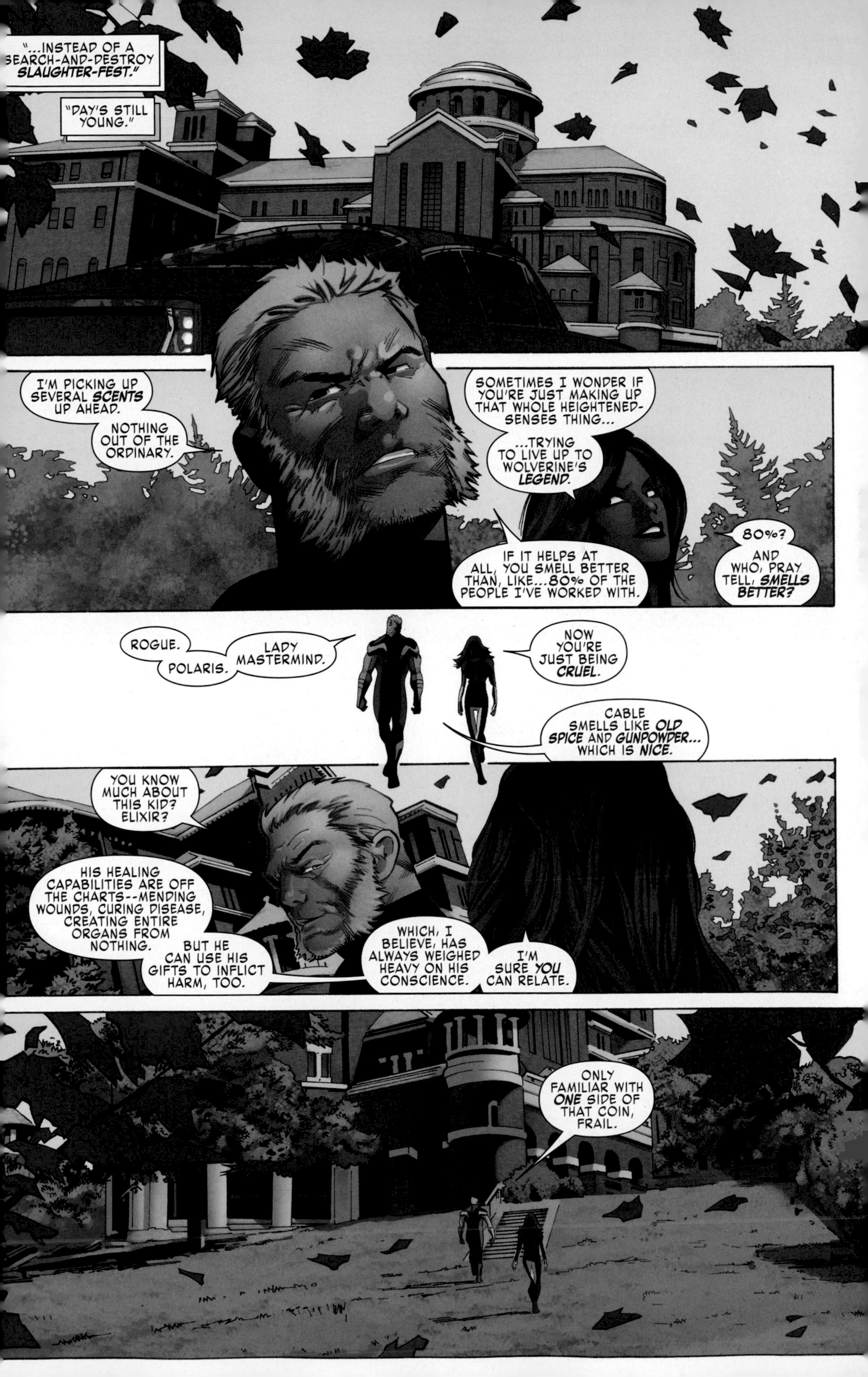
"...INSTEAD OF A SEARCH-AND-DESTROY SLAUGHTER-FEST."
"DAY'S STILL YOUNG."
I'M PICKING UP SEVERAL SCENTS UP AHEAD.
NOTHING OUT OF THE ORDINARY.
SOMETIMES I WONDER IF YOU'RE JUST MAKING UP THAT WHOLE HEIGHTENED-SENSES THING...
...TRYING TO LIVE UP TO WOLVERINE'S LEGEND.
IF IT HELPS AT ALL, YOU SMELL BETTER THAN, LIKE...80% OF THE PEOPLE I'VE WORKED WITH.
80%?
AND WHO, PRAY TELL, SMELLS BETTER?
ROGUE.
POLARIS.
LADY MASTERMIND.
NOW YOU'RE JUST BEING CRUEL.
CABLE SMELLS LIKE OLD SPICE AND GUNPOWDER... WHICH IS NICE.
YOU KNOW MUCH ABOUT THIS KID? ELIXIR?
HIS HEALING CAPABILITIES ARE OFF THE CHARTS--MENDING WOUNDS, CURING DISEASE, CREATING ENTIRE ORGANS FROM NOTHING.
BUT HE CAN USE HIS GIFTS TO INFLICT HARM, TOO.
WHICH, I BELIEVE, HAS ALWAYS WEIGHED HEAVY ON HIS CONSCIENCE.
I'M SURE YOU CAN RELATE.
ONLY FAMILIAR WITH ONE SIDE OF THAT COIN, FRAIL.

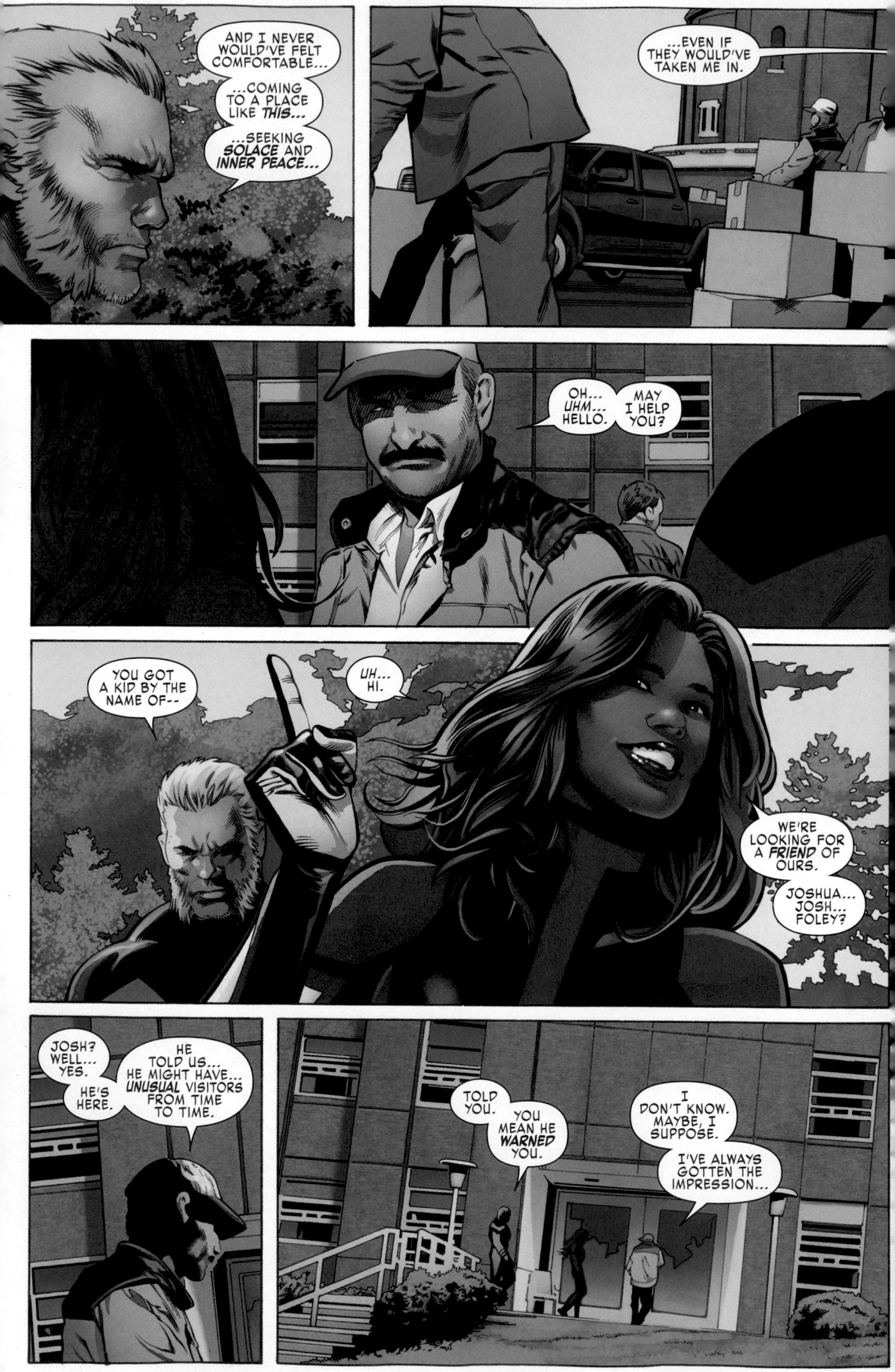
AND I NEVER WOULD'VE FELT COMFORTABLE...
...COMING TO A PLACE LIKE THIS...
...SEEKING SOLACE AND INNER PEACE...
...EVEN IF THEY WOULD'VE TAKEN ME IN.
OH... UHM... HELLO.
MAY I HELP YOU?
YOU GOT A KID BY THE NAME OF--
UH... HI.
WE'RE LOOKING FOR A FRIEND OF OURS.
JOSHUA... JOSH... FOLEY?
JOSH? WELL... YES.
HE'S HERE.
HE TOLD US... HE MIGHT HAVE... UNUSUAL VISITORS FROM TIME TO TIME.
TOLD YOU.
YOU MEAN HE WARNED YOU.
I DON'T KNOW. MAYBE, I SUPPOSE.
I'VE ALWAYS GOTTEN THE IMPRESSION...

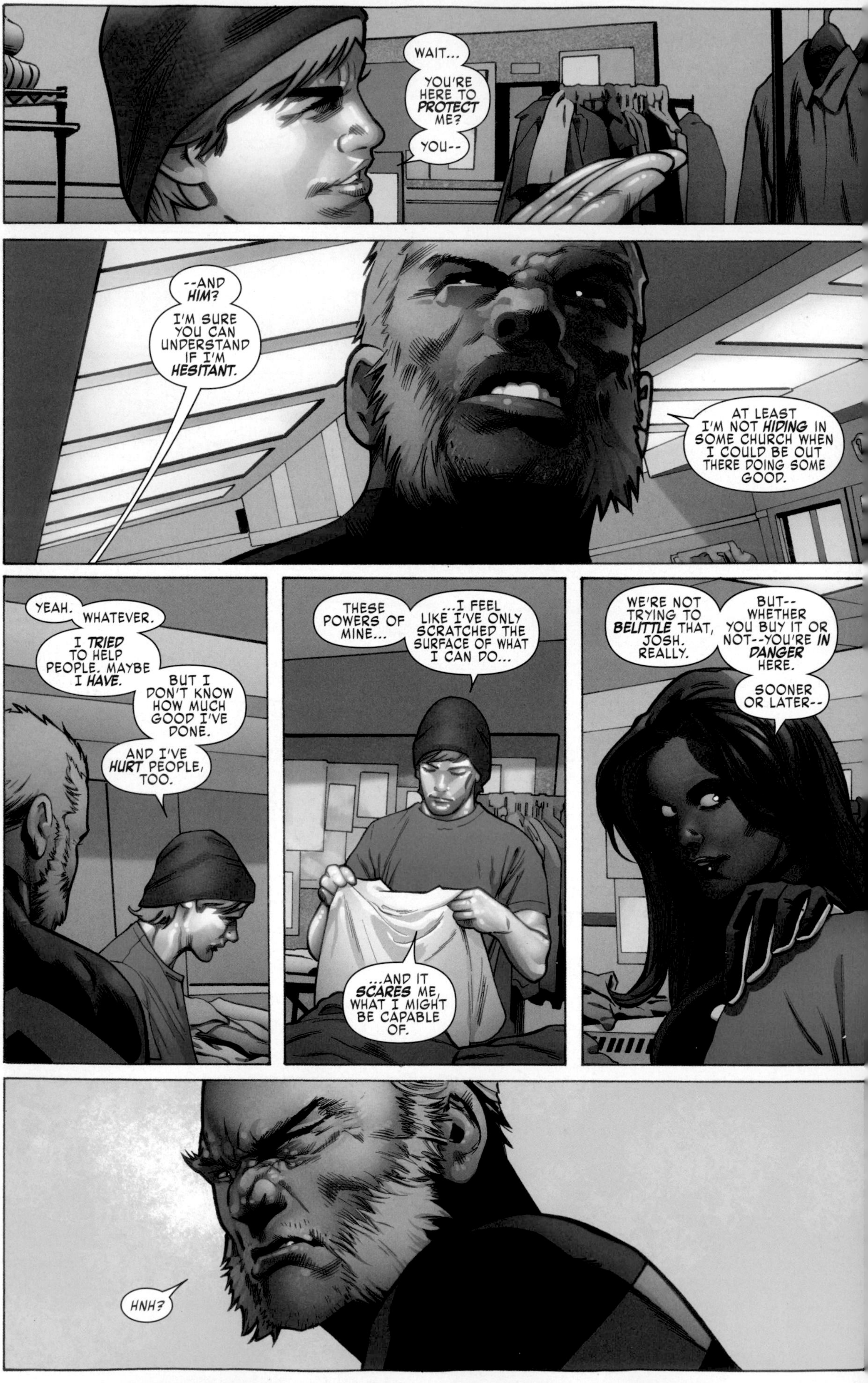
WAIT...
YOU'RE HERE TO *PROTECT* ME?
YOU--
--AND *HIM?*
I'M SURE YOU CAN UNDERSTAND IF I'M *HESITANT.*
AT LEAST I'M NOT *HIDING* IN SOME CHURCH WHEN I COULD BE OUT THERE DOING SOME GOOD.
YEAH.
WHATEVER.
I *TRIED* TO HELP PEOPLE. MAYBE I *HAVE.*
BUT I DON'T KNOW HOW MUCH GOOD I'VE DONE.
AND I'VE *HURT* PEOPLE, TOO.
THESE POWERS OF MINE...
...I FEEL LIKE I'VE ONLY SCRATCHED THE SURFACE OF WHAT I CAN DO...
...AND IT *SCARES* ME, WHAT I MIGHT BE CAPABLE OF.
WE'RE NOT TRYING TO *BELITTLE* THAT, JOSH. REALLY.
BUT--WHETHER YOU BUY IT OR NOT--YOU'RE *IN DANGER* HERE.
SOONER OR LATER--
HNH?

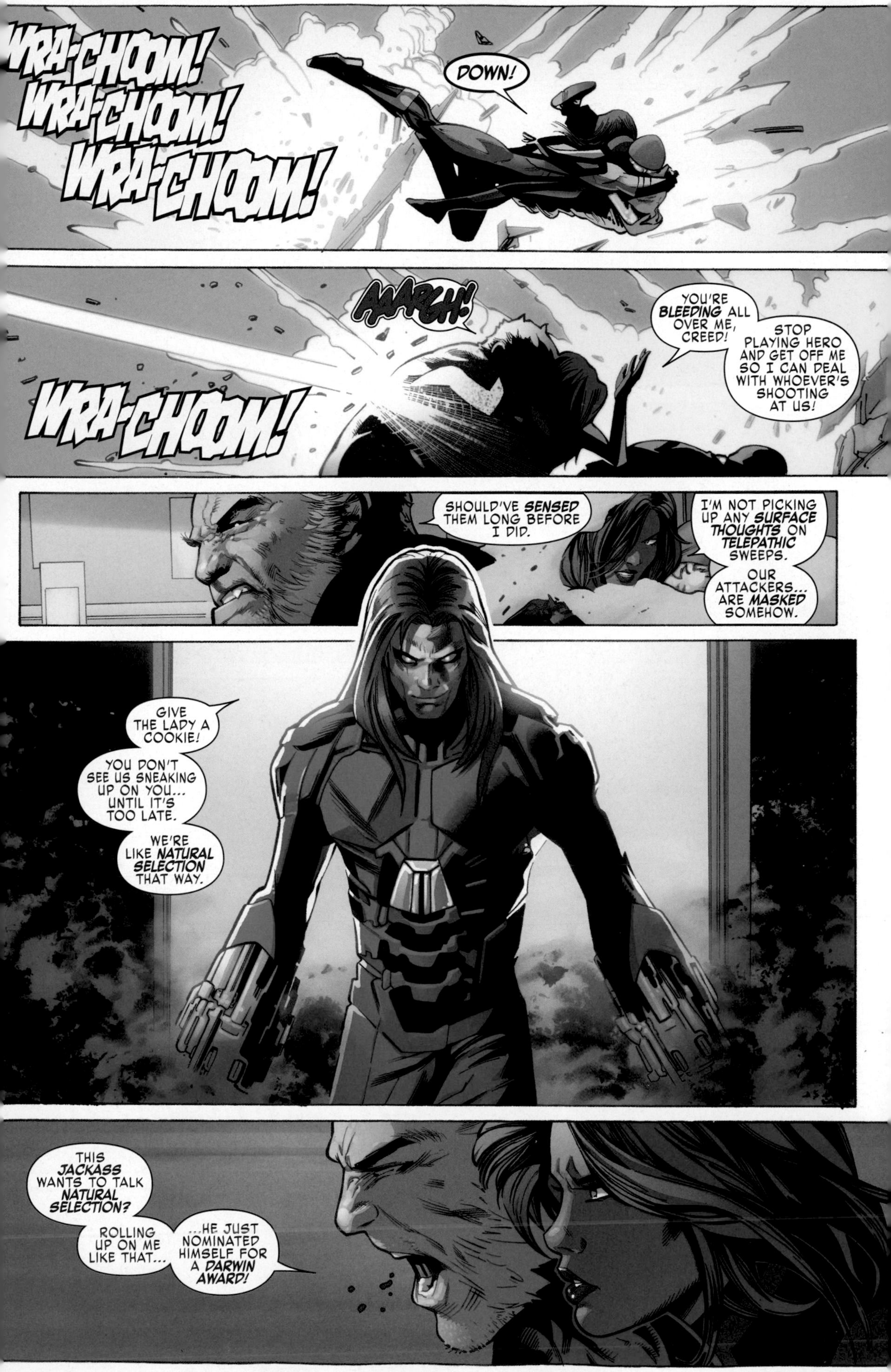
WRA-CHOOM!
WRA-CHOOM!
WRA-CHOOM!
DOWN!
AAARGH!
WRA-CHOOM!
YOU'RE BLEEDING ALL OVER ME, CREED!
STOP PLAYING HERO AND GET OFF ME SO I CAN DEAL WITH WHOEVER'S SHOOTING AT US!
SHOULD'VE SENSED THEM LONG BEFORE I DID.
I'M NOT PICKING UP ANY SURFACE THOUGHTS ON TELEPATHIC SWEEPS.
OUR ATTACKERS... ARE MASKED SOMEHOW.
GIVE THE LADY A COOKIE!
YOU DON'T SEE US SNEAKING UP ON YOU... UNTIL IT'S TOO LATE.
WE'RE LIKE NATURAL SELECTION THAT WAY.
THIS JACKASS WANTS TO TALK NATURAL SELECTION?
ROLLING UP ON ME LIKE THAT...
...HE JUST NOMINATED HIMSELF FOR A DARWIN AWARD!

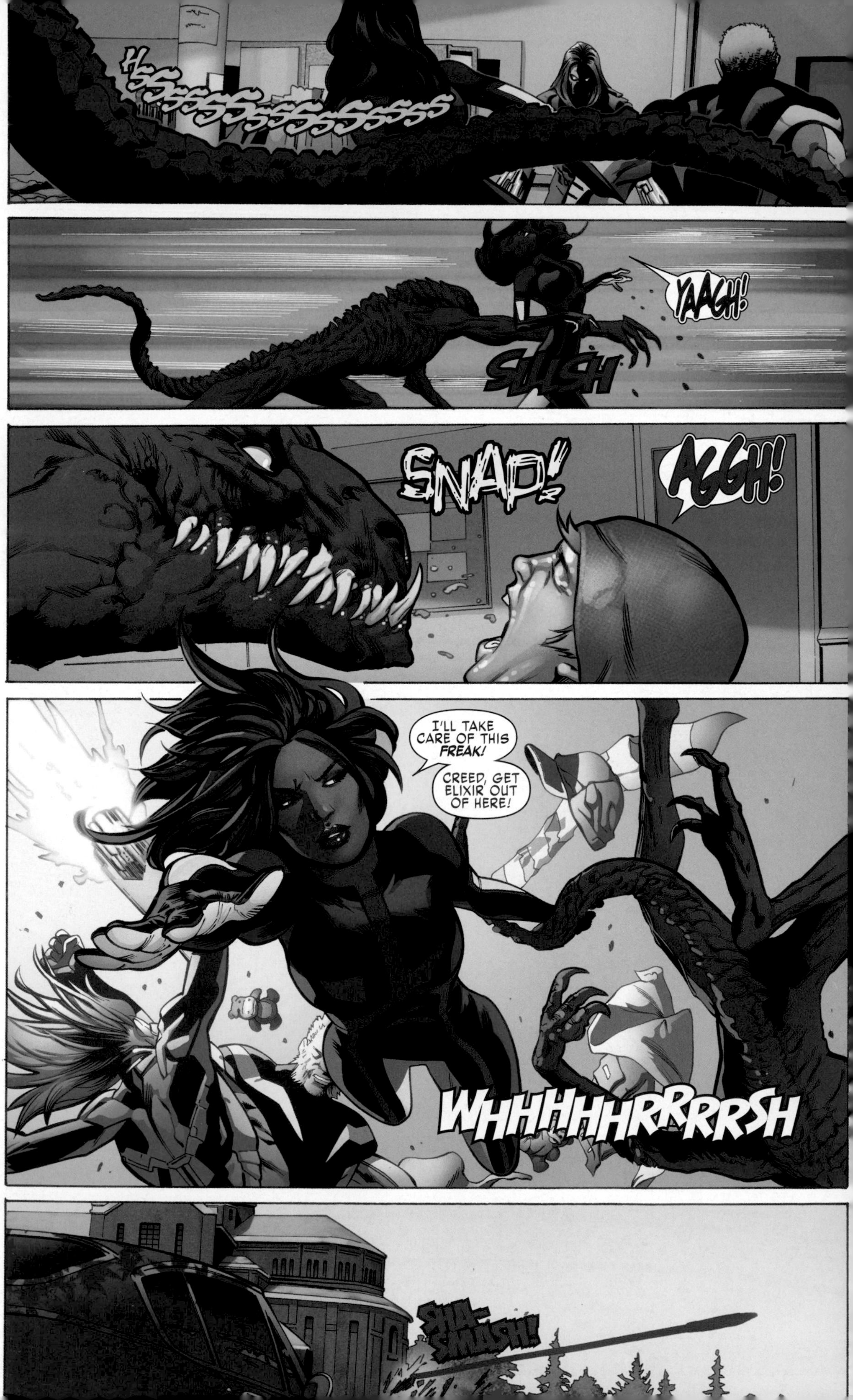
HSSSSSSSSSSSSSSSSS
YAAGH!
SHLUSH
SNAP!
AGGH!
I'LL TAKE CARE OF THIS FREAK!
CREED, GET ELIXIR OUT OF HERE!
WHHHHHRRRRSH
SHA-SMASH!

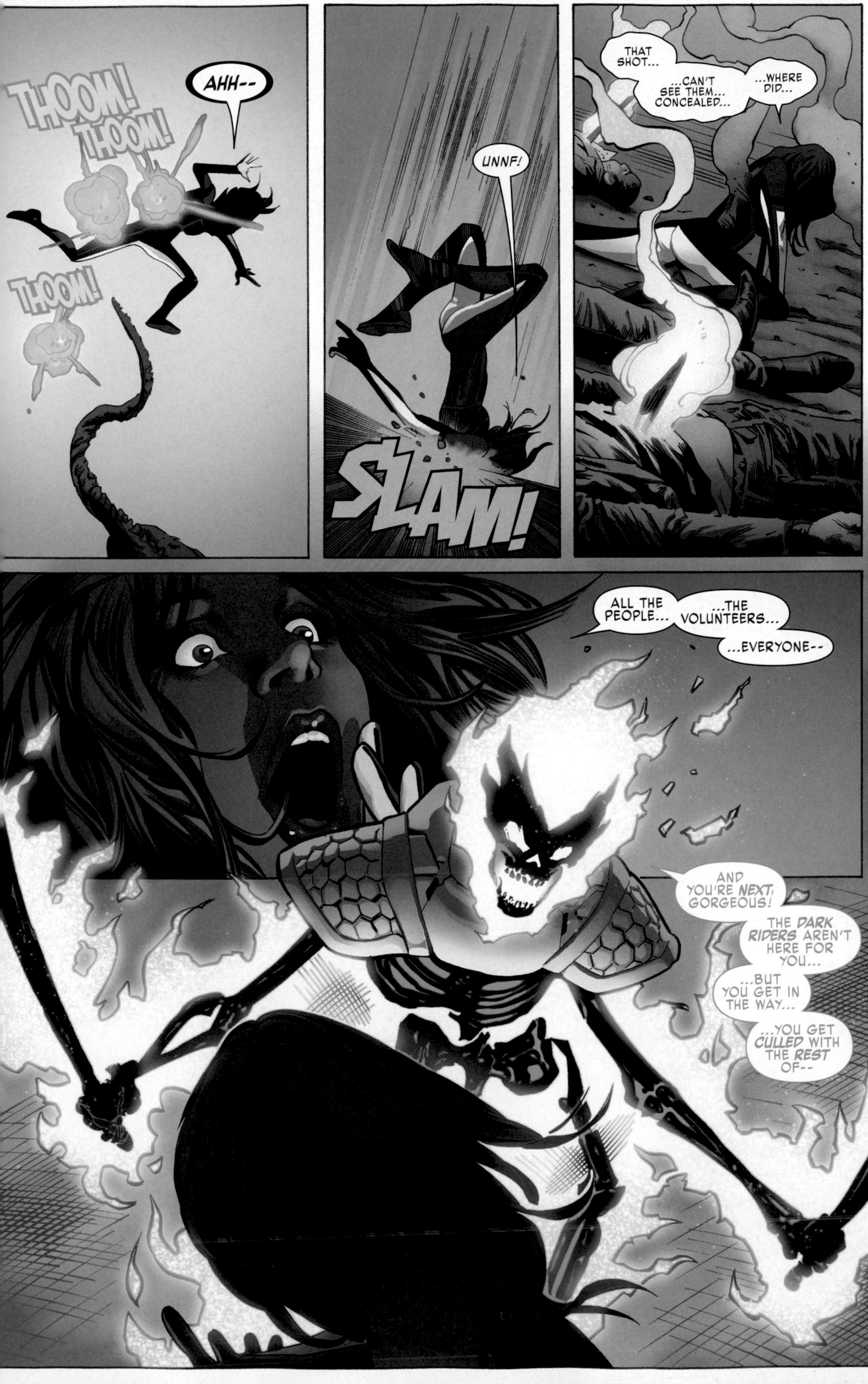
THOOM!
THOOM!
AHH--
THOOM!
UNNF!
SLAM!
THAT SHOT...
...CAN'T SEE THEM... CONCEALED...
...WHERE DID...
ALL THE PEOPLE...
...THE VOLUNTEERS...
...EVERYONE--
AND YOU'RE NEXT, GORGEOUS!
THE DARK RIDERS AREN'T HERE FOR YOU...
...BUT YOU GET IN THE WAY...
...YOU GET CULLED WITH THE REST OF--

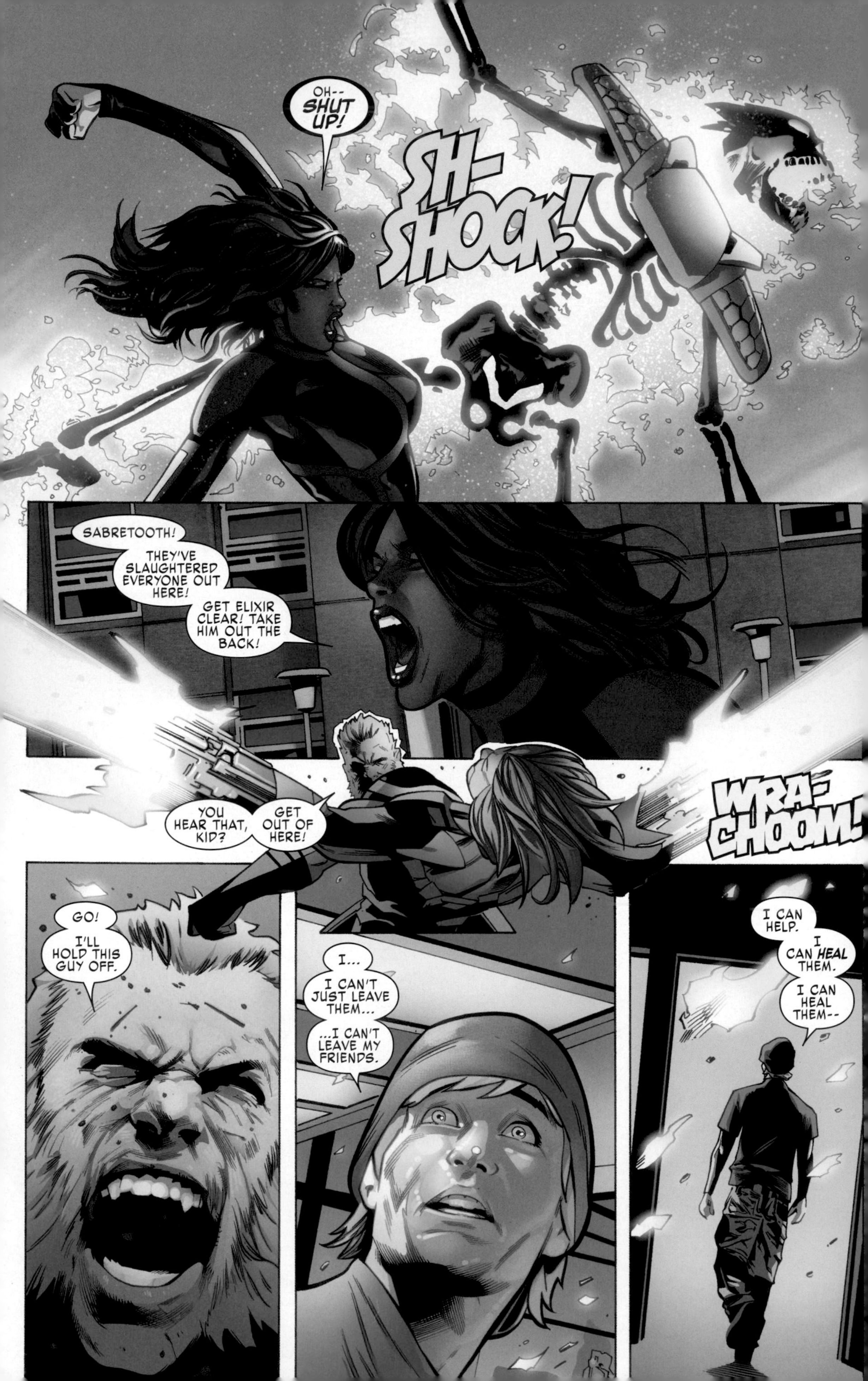
OH-- SHUT UP!
SH-SHOCK!
SABRETOOTH!
THEY'VE SLAUGHTERED EVERYONE OUT HERE!
GET ELIXIR CLEAR! TAKE HIM OUT THE BACK!
YOU HEAR THAT, KID?
GET OUT OF HERE!
WRA-CHOOM!
GO!
I'LL HOLD THIS GUY OFF.
I...
I CAN'T JUST LEAVE THEM...
...I CAN'T LEAVE MY FRIENDS.
I CAN HELP.
I CAN HEAL THEM.
I CAN HEAL THEM--

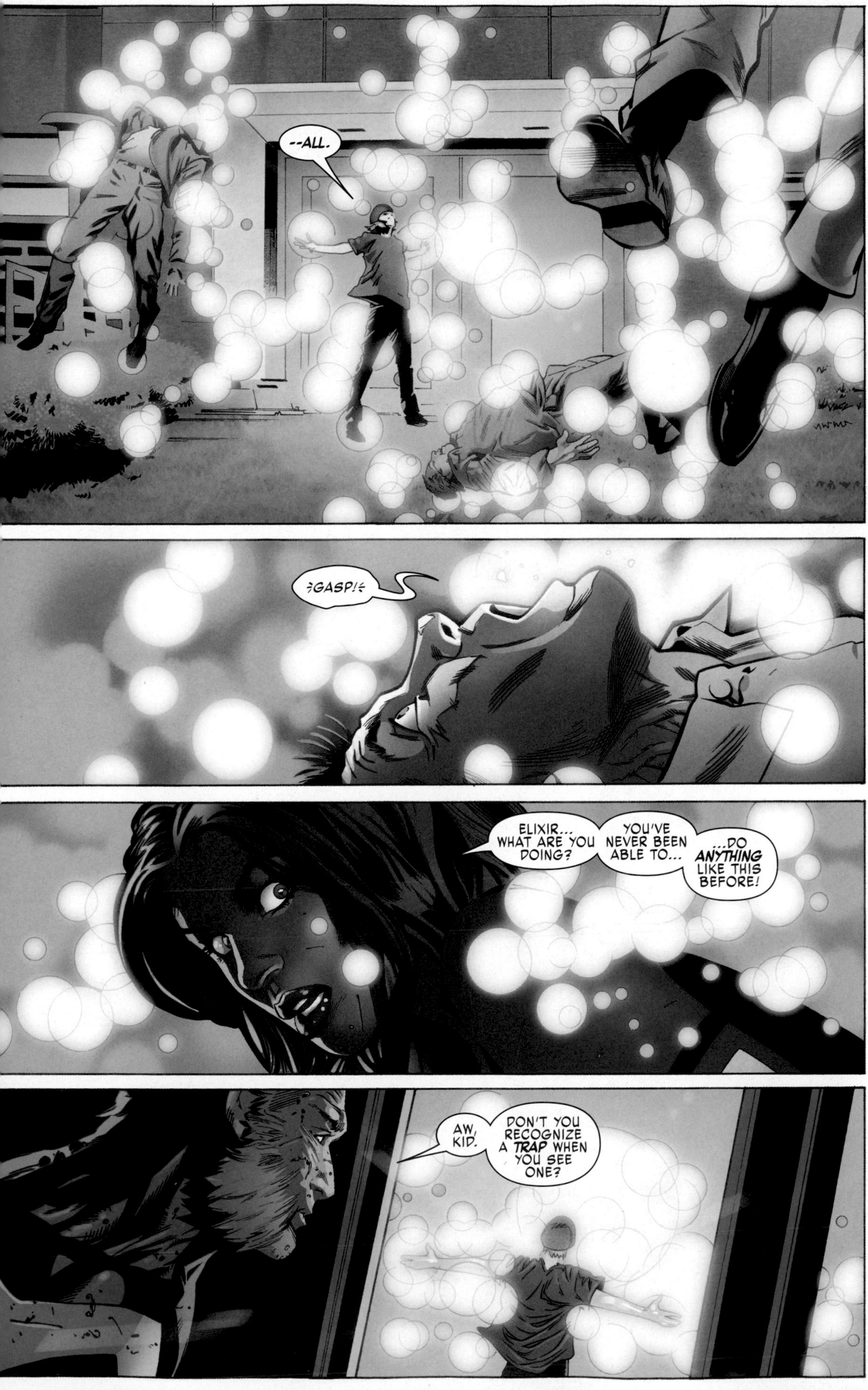
--ALL.
⋠GASP!⋡
ELIXIR... WHAT ARE YOU DOING?
YOU'VE NEVER BEEN ABLE TO...
...DO ANYTHING LIKE THIS BEFORE!
AW, KID.
DON'T YOU RECOGNIZE A TRAP WHEN YOU SEE ONE?

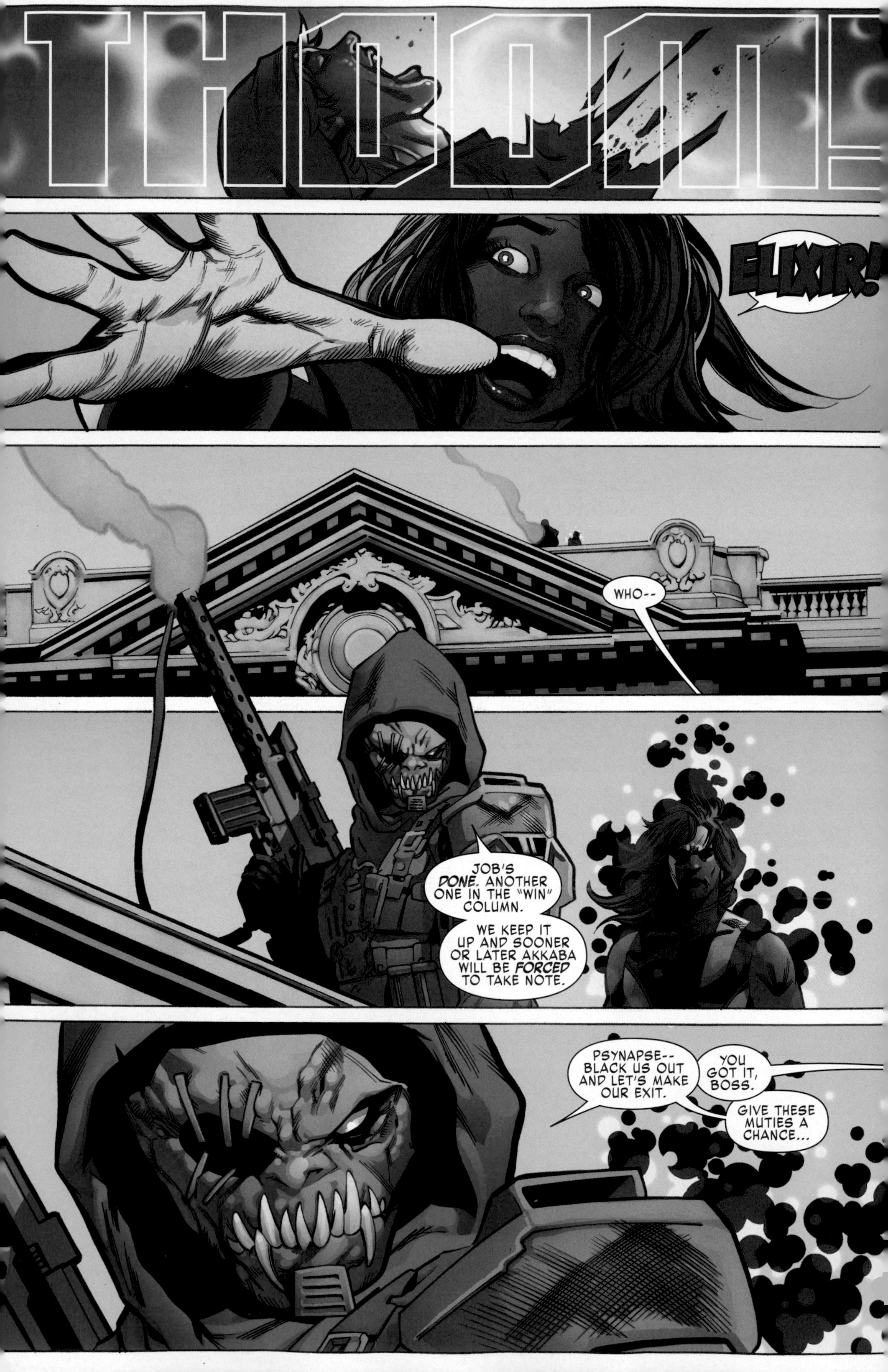

THOOM!
ELIXIR!
WHO--
JOB'S DONE. ANOTHER ONE IN THE "WIN" COLUMN.
WE KEEP IT UP AND SOONER OR LATER AKKABA WILL BE FORCED TO TAKE NOTE.
PSYNAPSE-- BLACK US OUT AND LET'S MAKE OUR EXIT.
YOU GOT IT, BOSS.
GIVE THESE MUTIES A CHANCE...

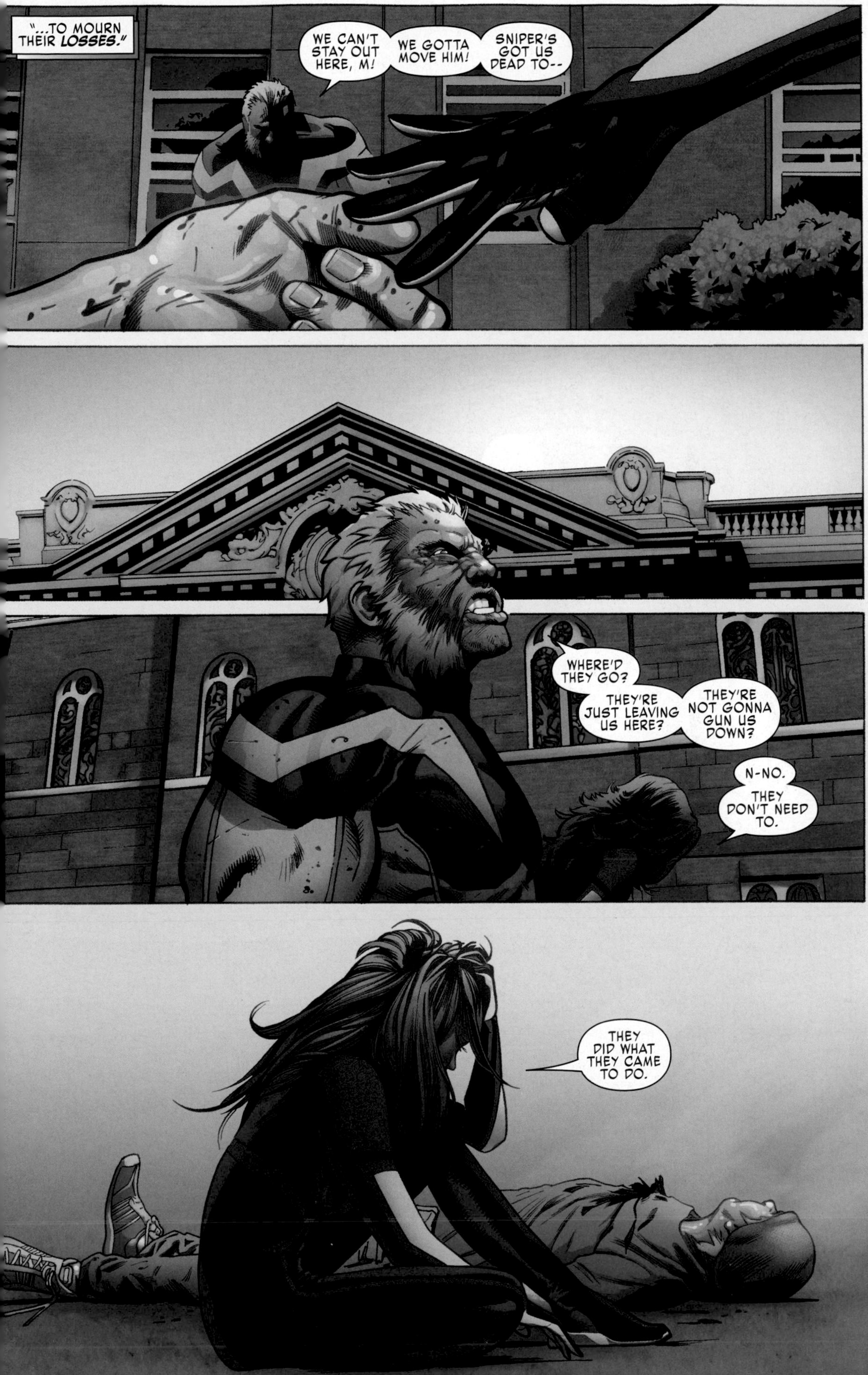
"...TO MOURN THEIR *LOSSES.*"
WE CAN'T STAY OUT HERE, M!
WE GOTTA MOVE HIM!
SNIPER'S GOT US DEAD TO--
WHERE'D THEY GO?
THEY'RE JUST LEAVING US HERE?
THEY'RE NOT GONNA GUN US DOWN?
N-NO.
THEY DON'T NEED TO.
THEY DID WHAT THEY CAME TO DO.

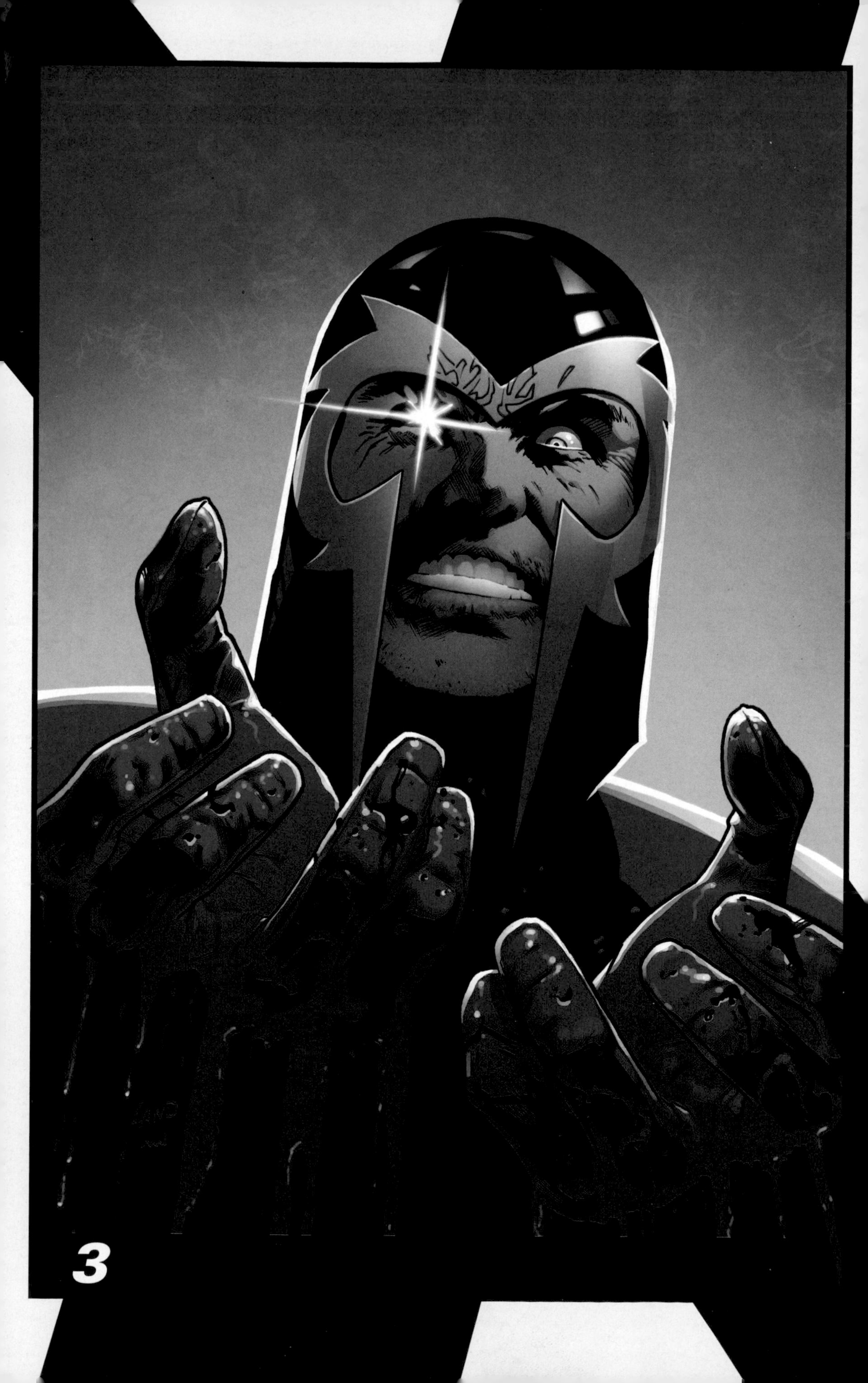
3

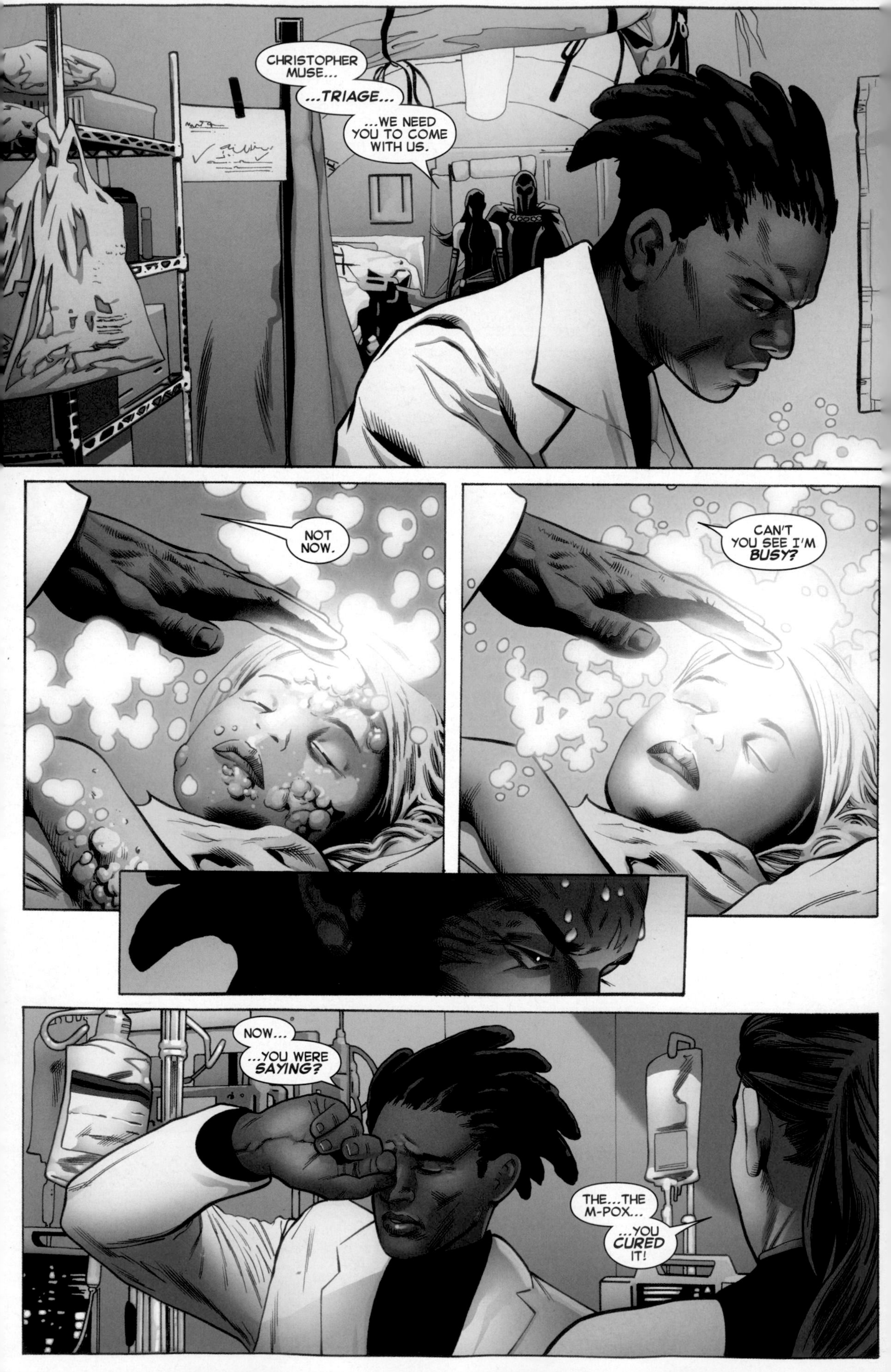
CHRISTOPHER MUSE...
...TRIAGE...
...WE NEED YOU TO COME WITH US.
NOT NOW.
CAN'T YOU SEE I'M BUSY?
NOW...
...YOU WERE SAYING?
THE...THE M-POX...
...YOU CURED IT!

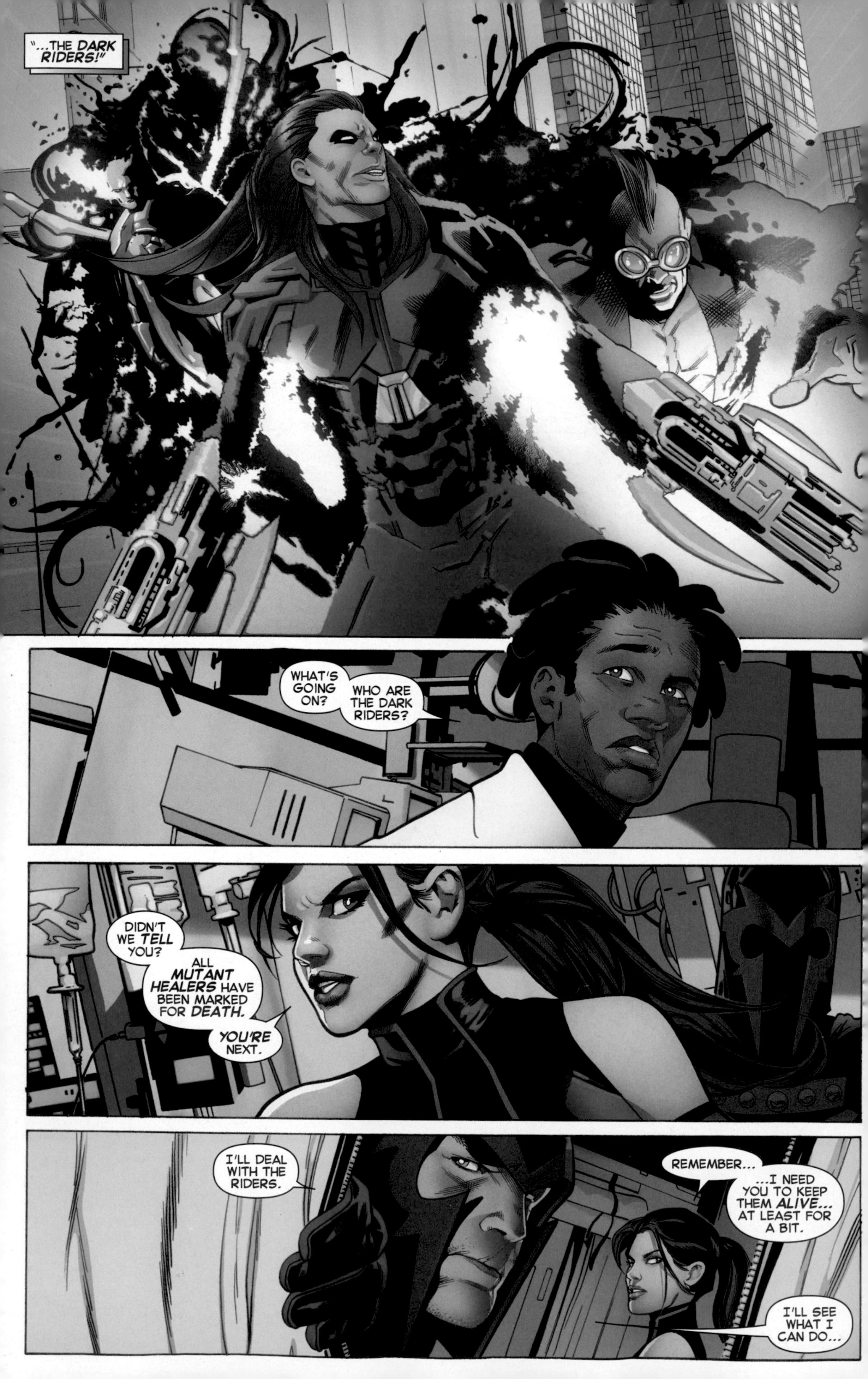
"...THE DARK RIDERS!"
WHAT'S GOING ON?
WHO ARE THE DARK RIDERS?
DIDN'T WE TELL YOU?
ALL MUTANT HEALERS HAVE BEEN MARKED FOR DEATH.
YOU'RE NEXT.
I'LL DEAL WITH THE RIDERS.
REMEMBER...
...I NEED YOU TO KEEP THEM ALIVE... AT LEAST FOR A BIT.
I'LL SEE WHAT I CAN DO...

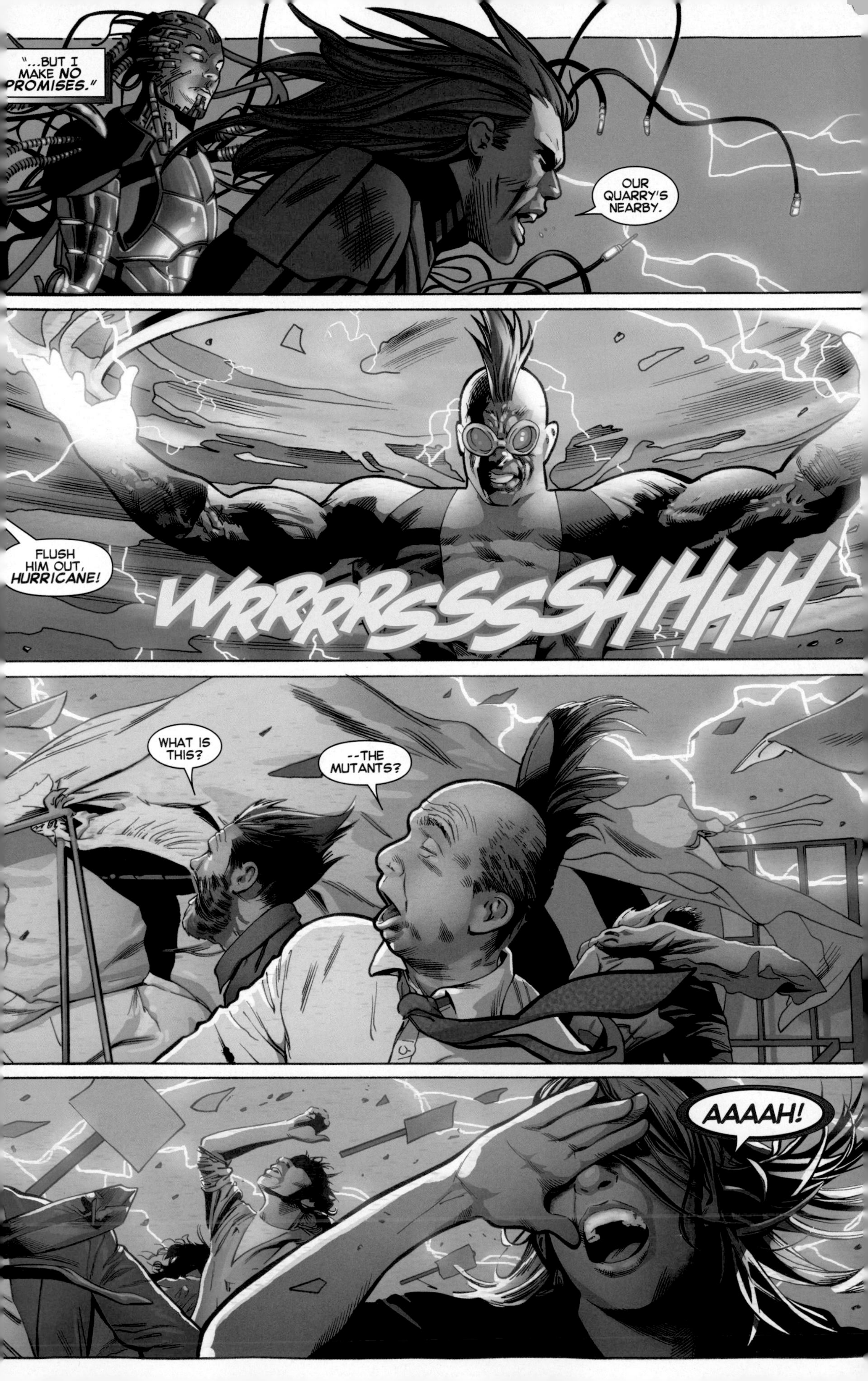
"...BUT I MAKE NO PROMISES."
OUR QUARRY'S NEARBY.
FLUSH HIM OUT, HURRICANE!
WRRRRSSSSHHHH
WHAT IS THIS?
--THE MUTANTS?
AAAAH!

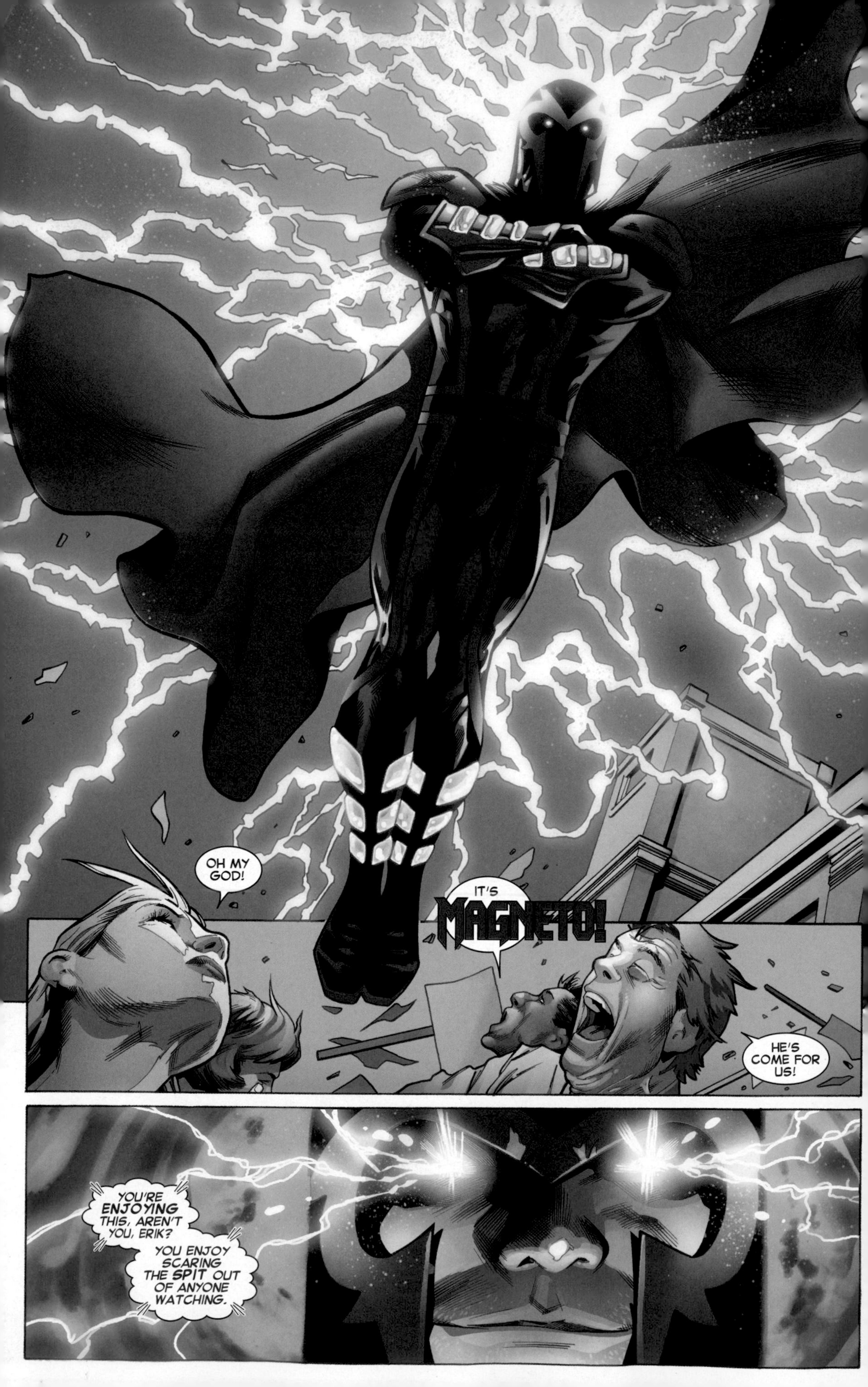
OH MY GOD!
IT'S MAGNETO!
HE'S COME FOR US!
YOU'RE ENJOYING THIS, AREN'T YOU, ERIK?
YOU ENJOY SCARING THE SPIT OUT OF ANYONE WATCHING.

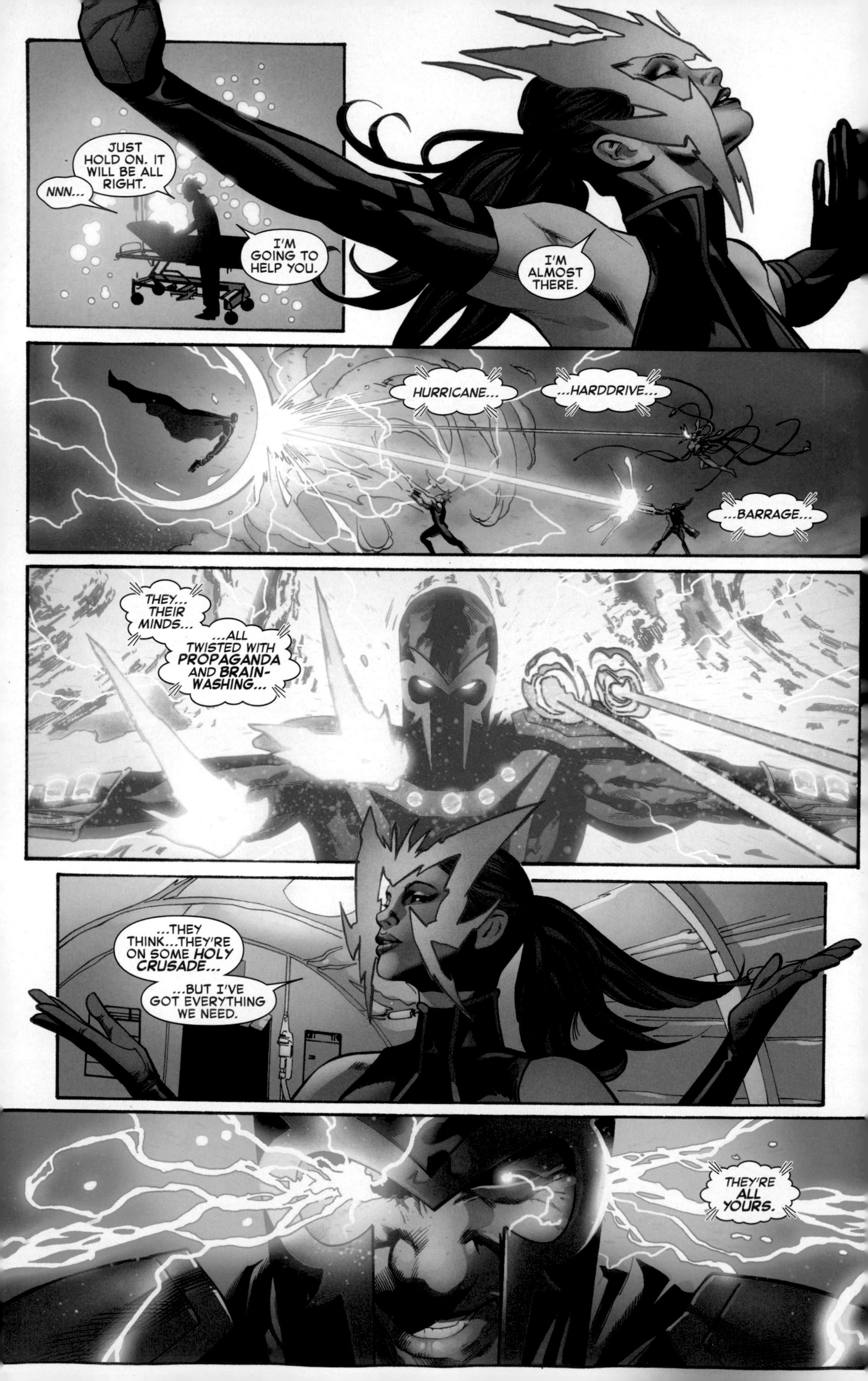
JUST HOLD ON. IT WILL BE ALL RIGHT.
NNN...
I'M GOING TO HELP YOU.
I'M ALMOST THERE.
HURRICANE...
...HARDDRIVE...
...BARRAGE...
THEY... THEIR MINDS...
...ALL TWISTED WITH PROPAGANDA AND BRAIN-WASHING...
...THEY THINK...THEY'RE ON SOME HOLY CRUSADE...
...BUT I'VE GOT EVERYTHING WE NEED.
THEY'RE ALL YOURS.

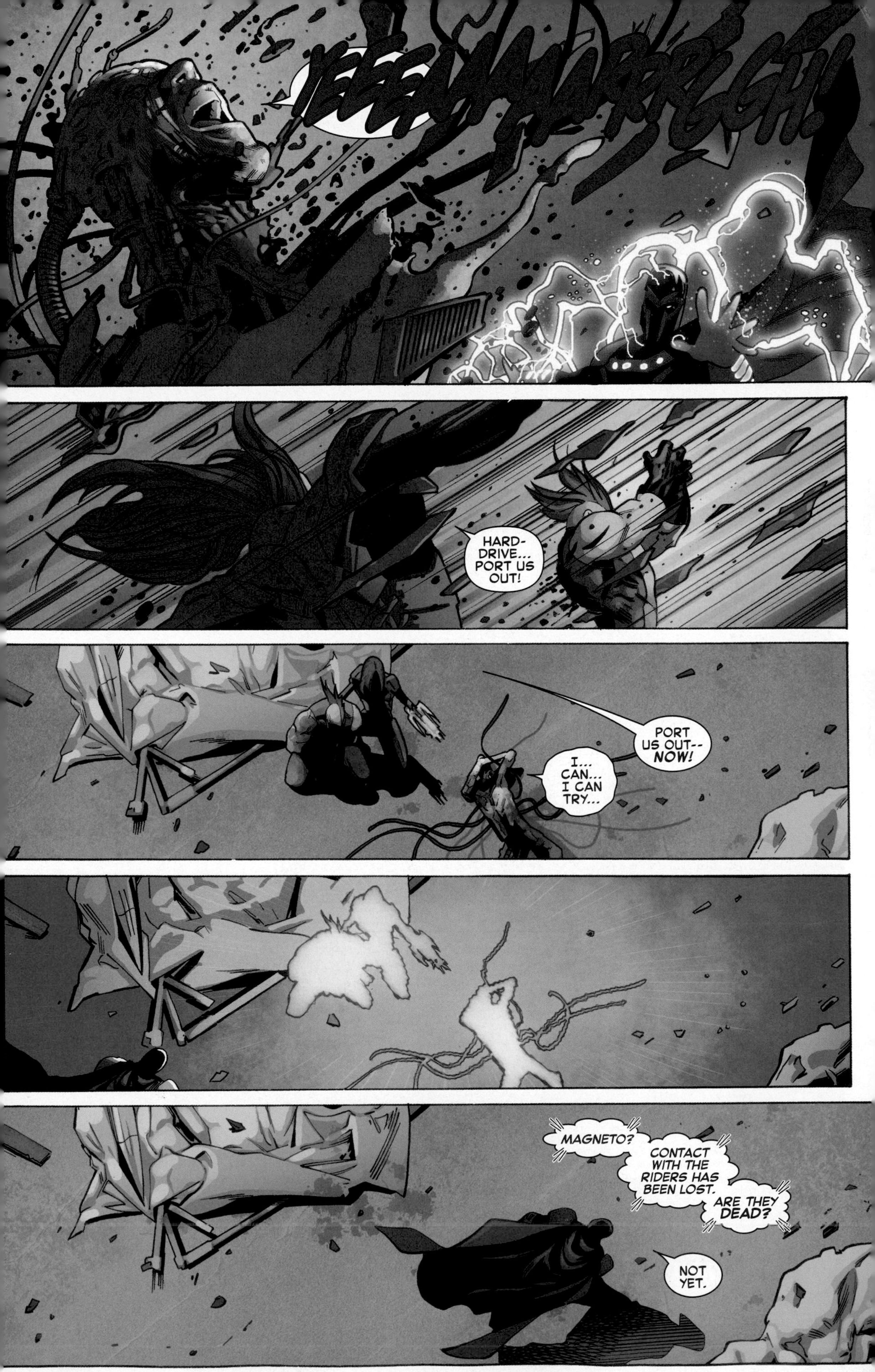
YEEEAAAAARRRGGH!
HARD-DRIVE... PORT US OUT!
PORT US OUT--NOW!
I... CAN... I CAN TRY...
MAGNETO?
CONTACT WITH THE RIDERS HAS BEEN LOST.
ARE THEY DEAD?
NOT YET.

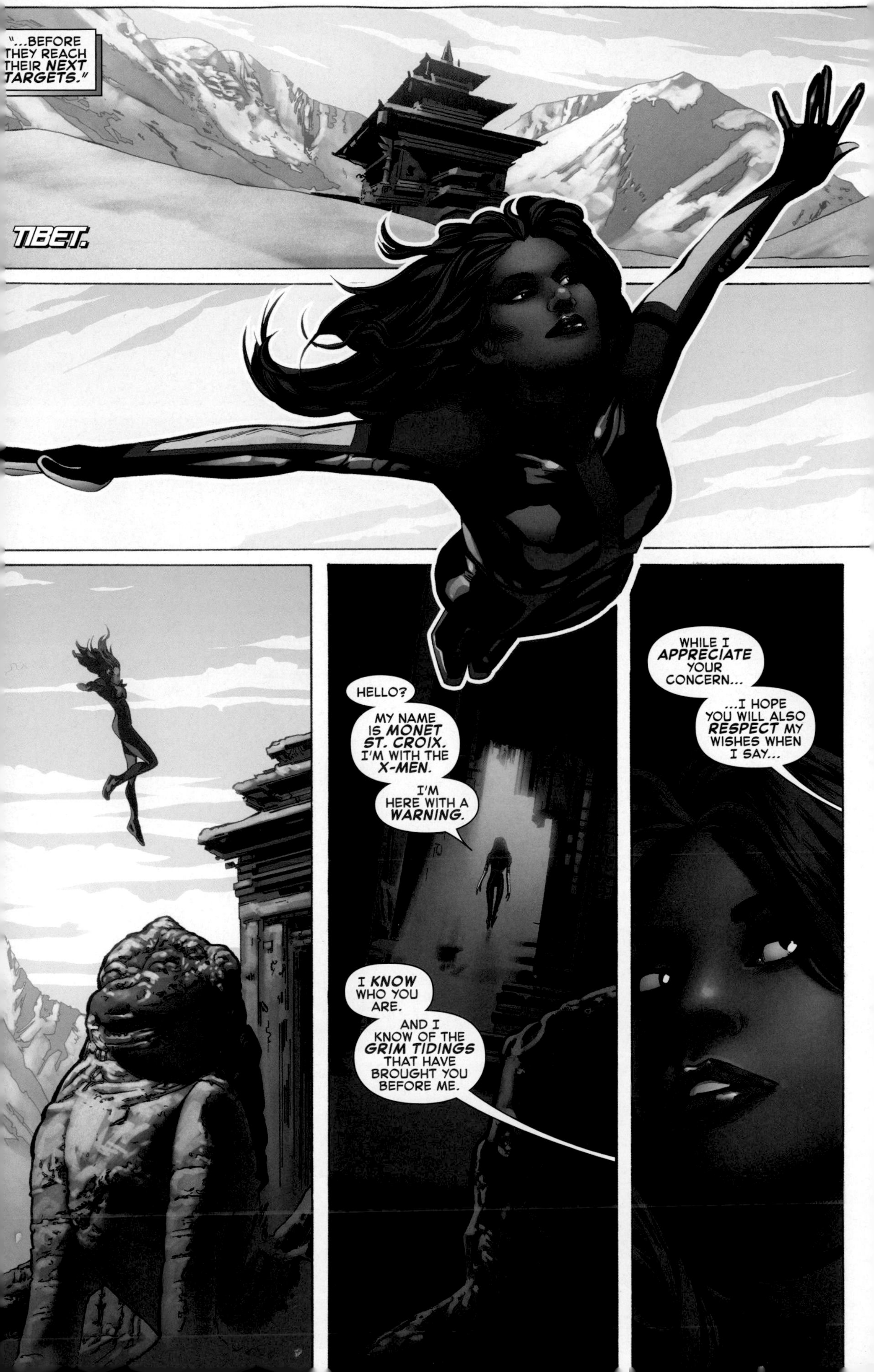
"...BEFORE THEY REACH THEIR NEXT TARGETS."
TIBET.
HELLO?
MY NAME IS MONET ST. CROIX. I'M WITH THE X-MEN.
I'M HERE WITH A WARNING.
I KNOW WHO YOU ARE.
AND I KNOW OF THE GRIM TIDINGS THAT HAVE BROUGHT YOU BEFORE ME.
WHILE I APPRECIATE YOUR CONCERN...
...I HOPE YOU WILL ALSO RESPECT MY WISHES WHEN I SAY...

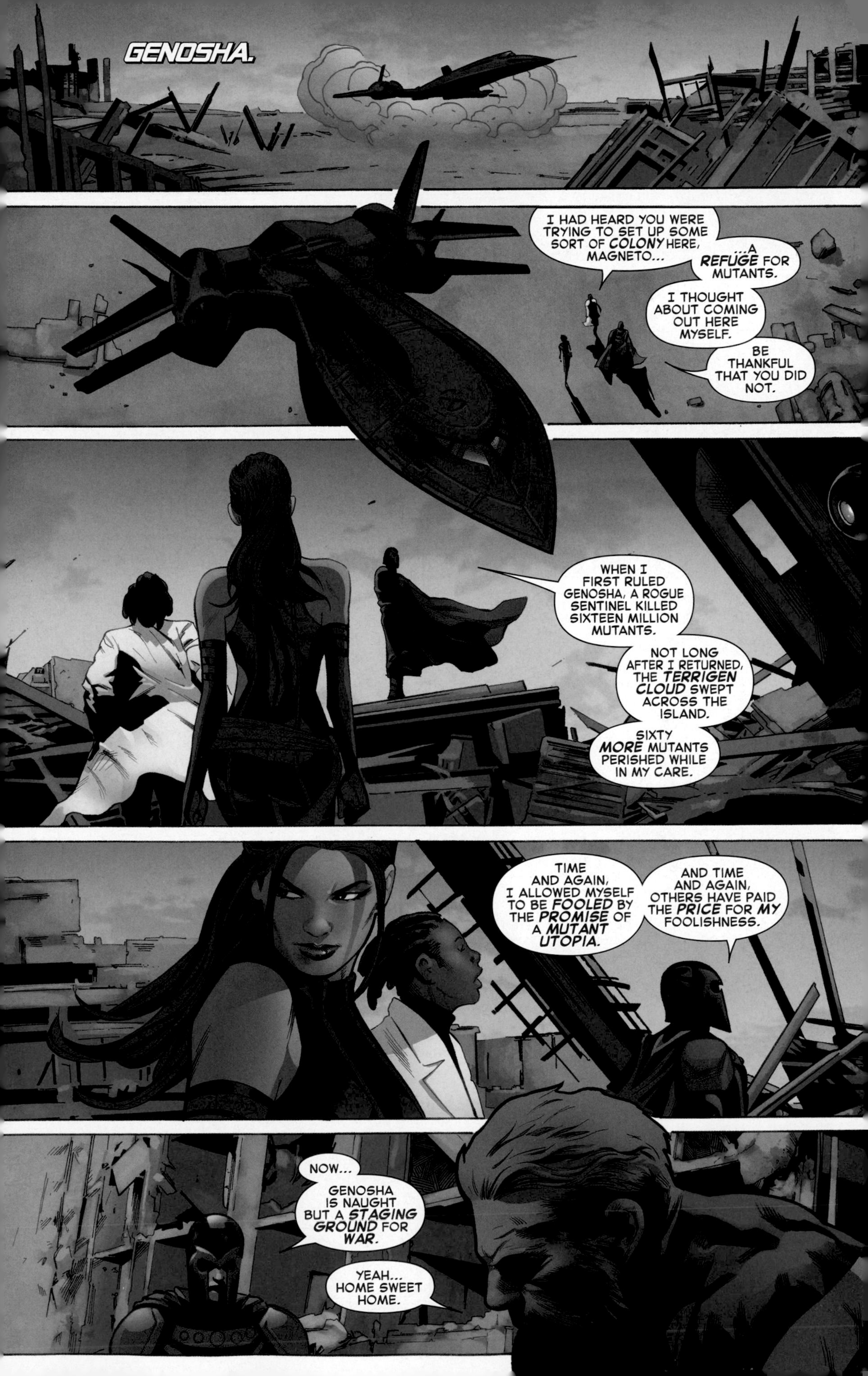
GENOSHA.
I HAD HEARD YOU WERE TRYING TO SET UP SOME SORT OF COLONY HERE, MAGNETO...
...A REFUGE FOR MUTANTS.
I THOUGHT ABOUT COMING OUT HERE MYSELF.
BE THANKFUL THAT YOU DID NOT.
WHEN I FIRST RULED GENOSHA, A ROGUE SENTINEL KILLED SIXTEEN MILLION MUTANTS.
NOT LONG AFTER I RETURNED, THE TERRIGEN CLOUD SWEPT ACROSS THE ISLAND.
SIXTY MORE MUTANTS PERISHED WHILE IN MY CARE.
TIME AND AGAIN, I ALLOWED MYSELF TO BE FOOLED BY THE PROMISE OF A MUTANT UTOPIA.
AND TIME AND AGAIN, OTHERS HAVE PAID THE PRICE FOR MY FOOLISHNESS.
NOW...
GENOSHA IS NAUGHT BUT A STAGING GROUND FOR WAR.
YEAH... HOME SWEET HOME.

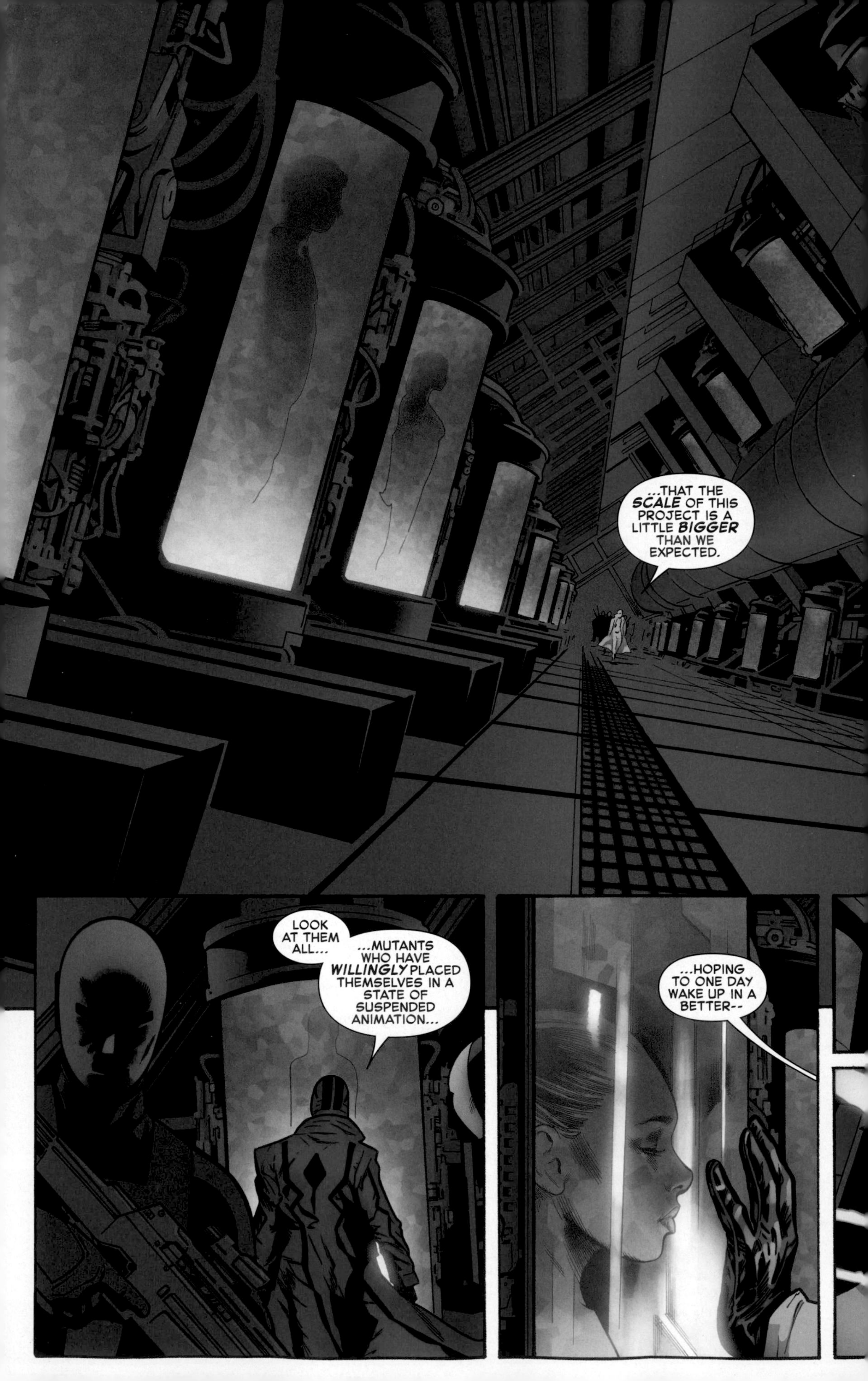

...THAT THE SCALE OF THIS PROJECT IS A LITTLE BIGGER THAN WE EXPECTED.
LOOK AT THEM ALL...
...MUTANTS WHO HAVE WILLINGLY PLACED THEMSELVES IN A STATE OF SUSPENDED ANIMATION...
...HOPING TO ONE DAY WAKE UP IN A BETTER--

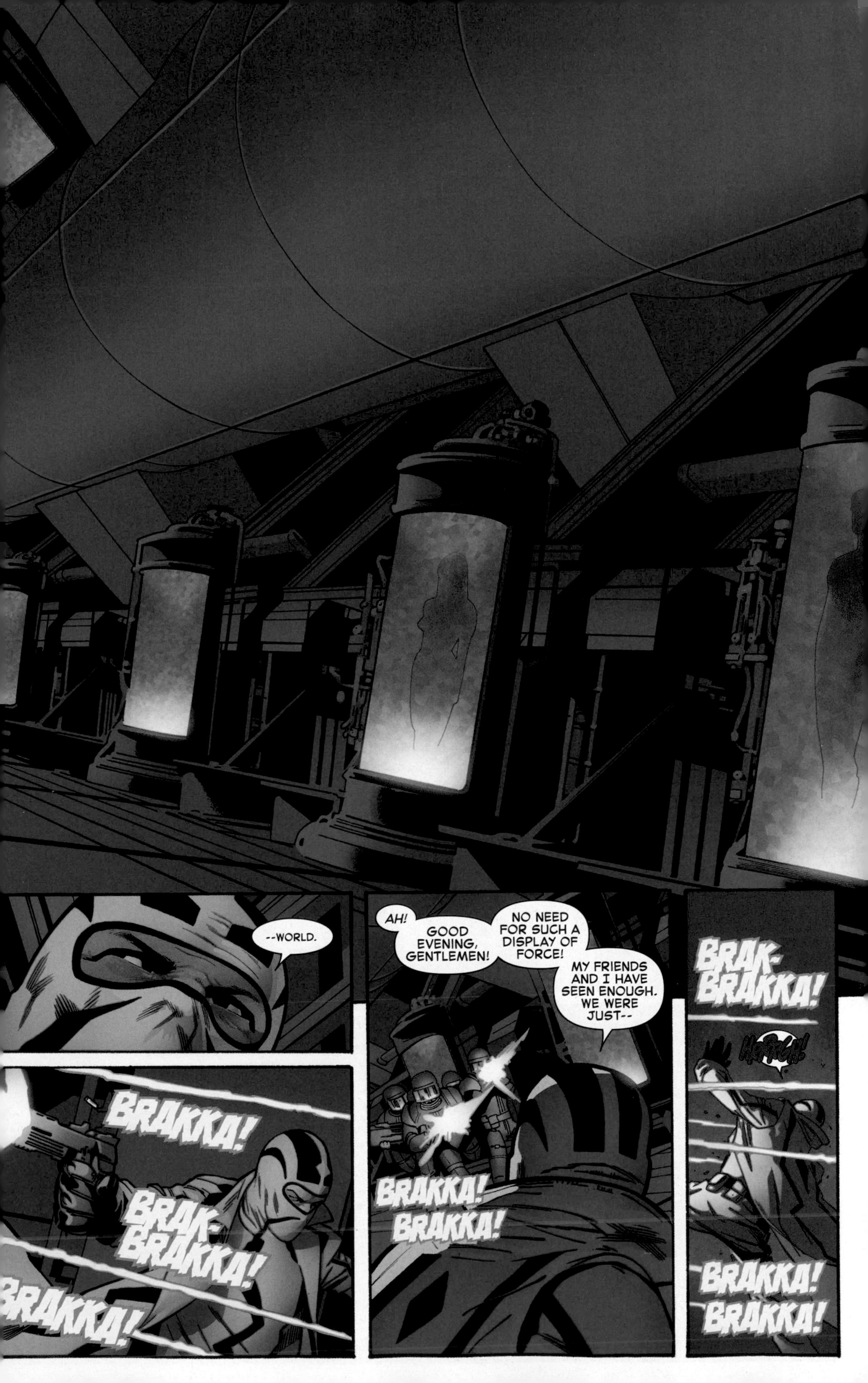
--WORLD.
BRAKKA!
BRAK-BRAKKA!
BRAKKA!
AH!
GOOD EVENING, GENTLEMEN!
NO NEED FOR SUCH A DISPLAY OF FORCE!
MY FRIENDS AND I HAVE SEEN ENOUGH. WE WERE JUST--
BRAKKA! BRAKKA!
BRAK-BRAKKA!
BRAKKA! BRAKKA!

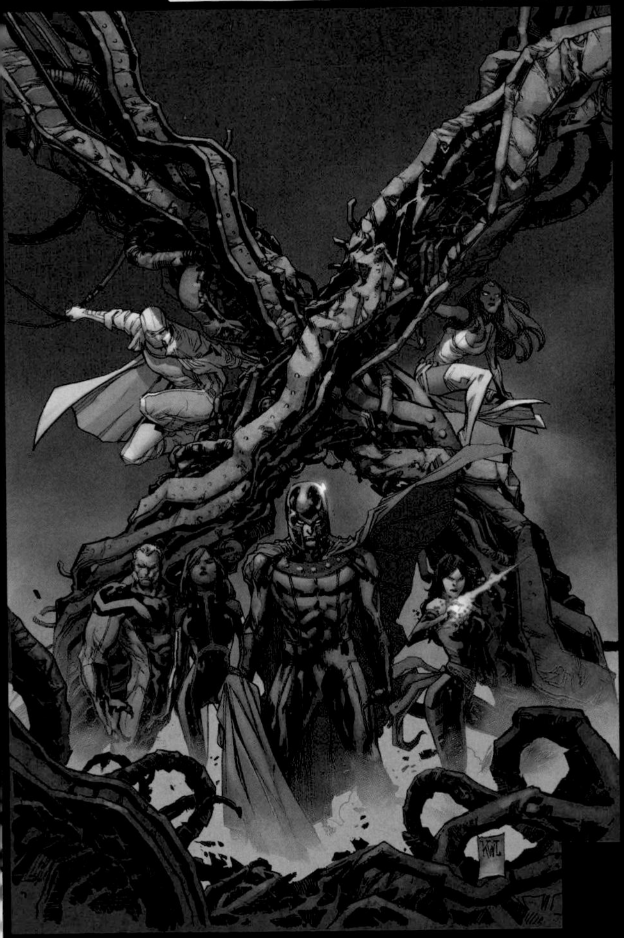

#1 VARIANT BY
KEN LASHLEY** & **NOLAN WOODARD

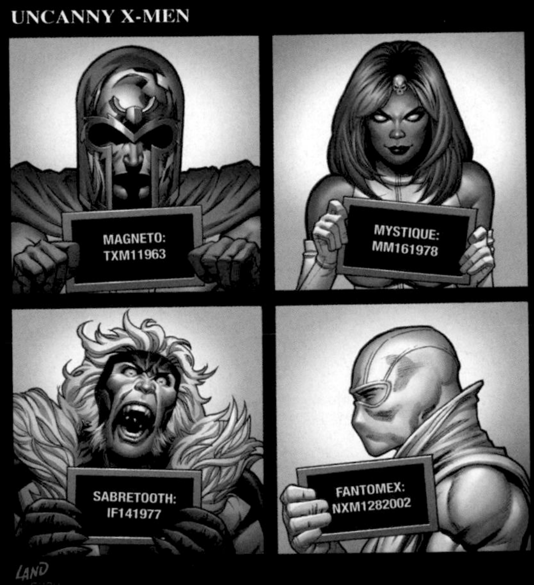
UNCANNY X-MEN
MAGNETO:
TXM11963
MYSTIQUE:
MM161978
SABRETOOTH:
IF141977
FANTOMEX:
NXM1282002
LAND

#1 HIP-HOP VARIANT BY
GREG LAND, JAY LEISTEN** & **GURU-eFX

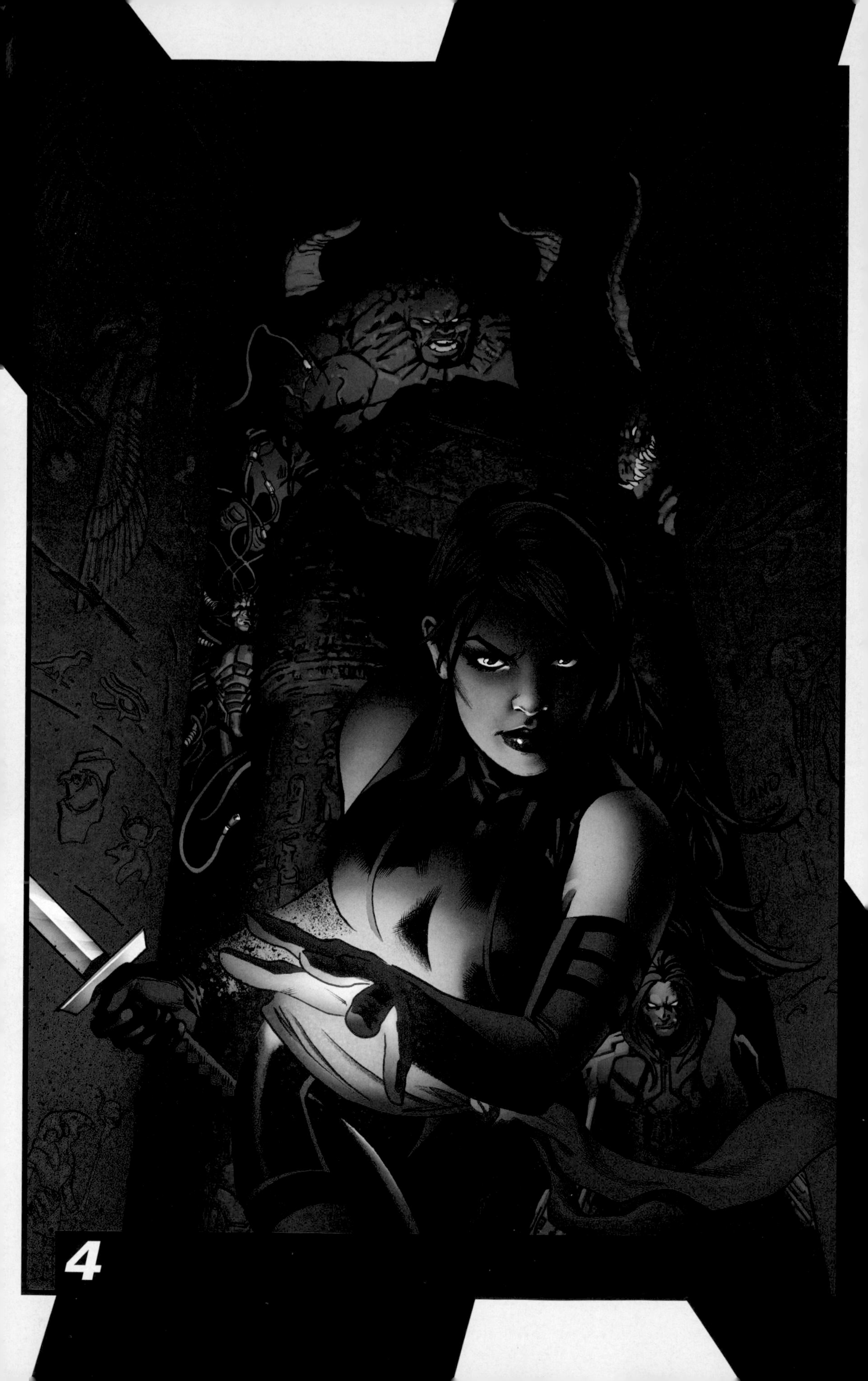
4

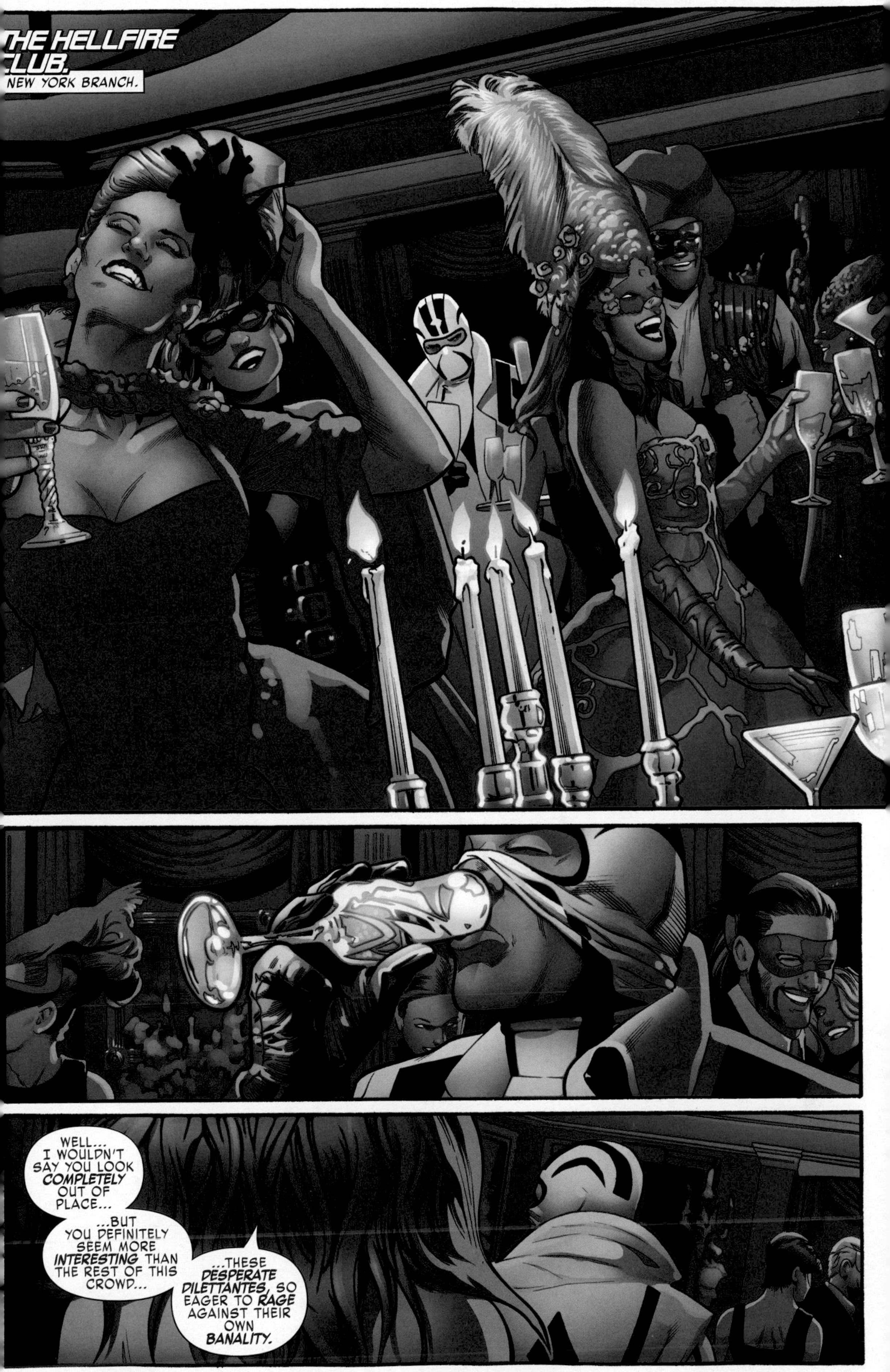
THE HELLFIRE CLUB.
NEW YORK BRANCH.
WELL... I WOULDN'T SAY YOU LOOK COMPLETELY OUT OF PLACE...
...BUT YOU DEFINITELY SEEM MORE INTERESTING THAN THE REST OF THIS CROWD...
...THESE DESPERATE DILETTANTES, SO EAGER TO RAGE AGAINST THEIR OWN BANALITY.

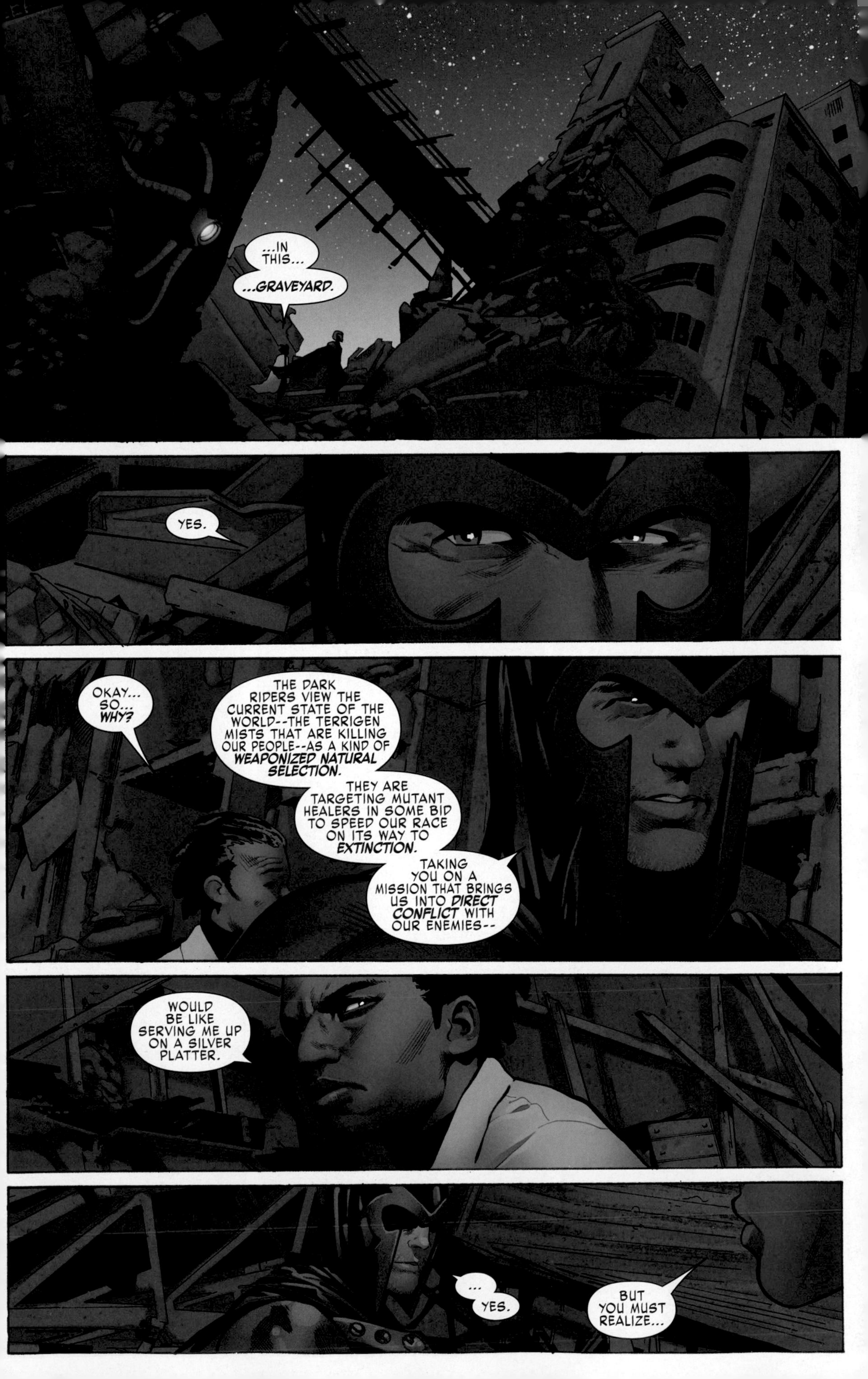
...IN THIS...
...GRAVEYARD.
YES.
OKAY... SO... WHY?
THE DARK RIDERS VIEW THE CURRENT STATE OF THE WORLD--THE TERRIGEN MISTS THAT ARE KILLING OUR PEOPLE--AS A KIND OF WEAPONIZED NATURAL SELECTION.
THEY ARE TARGETING MUTANT HEALERS IN SOME BID TO SPEED OUR RACE ON ITS WAY TO EXTINCTION.
TAKING YOU ON A MISSION THAT BRINGS US INTO DIRECT CONFLICT WITH OUR ENEMIES--
WOULD BE LIKE SERVING ME UP ON A SILVER PLATTER.
... YES.
BUT YOU MUST REALIZE...

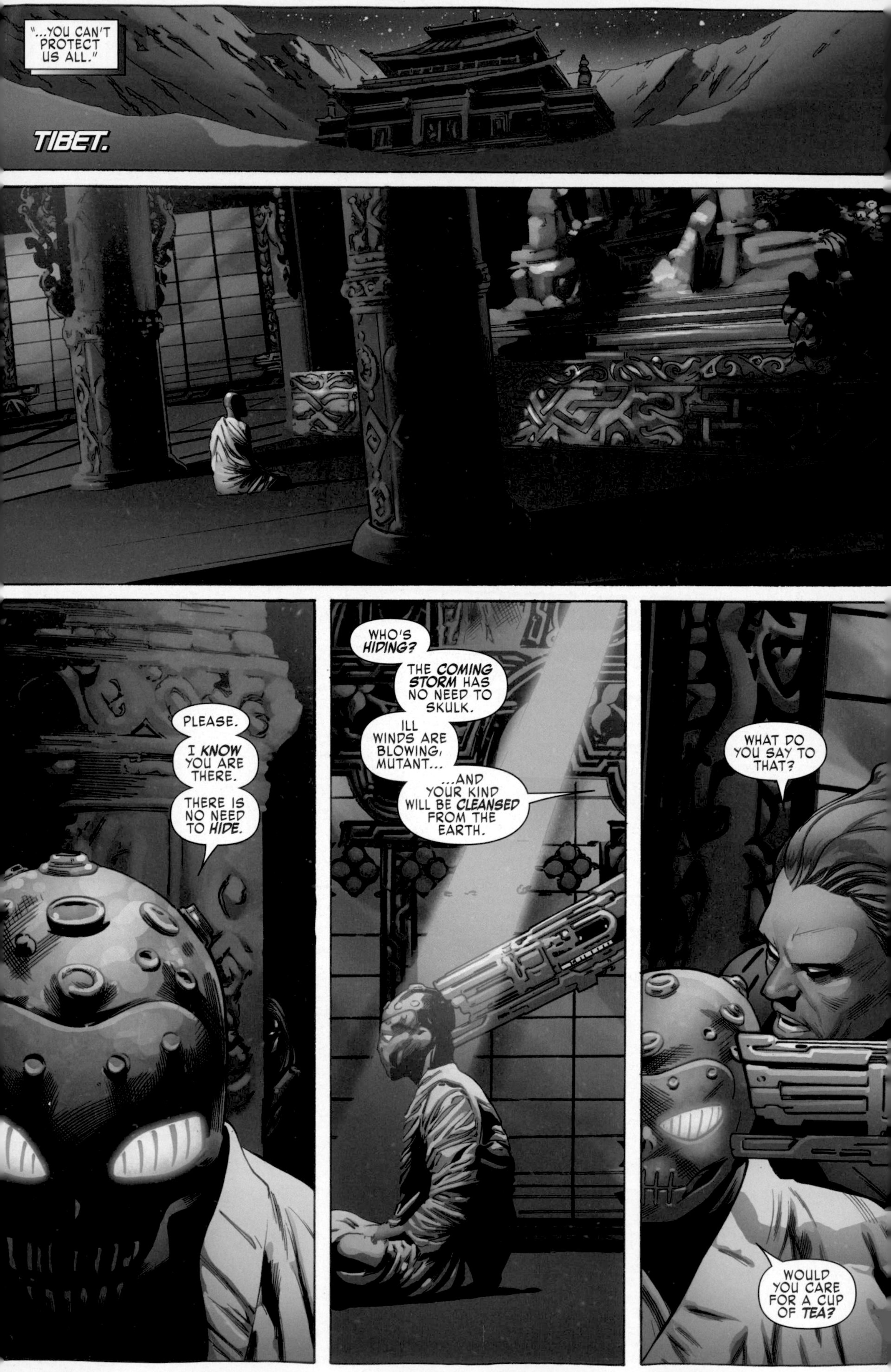
"...YOU CAN'T PROTECT US ALL."
TIBET.
PLEASE.
I KNOW YOU ARE THERE.
THERE IS NO NEED TO HIDE.
WHO'S HIDING?
THE COMING STORM HAS NO NEED TO SKULK.
ILL WINDS ARE BLOWING, MUTANT...
...AND YOUR KIND WILL BE CLEANSED FROM THE EARTH.
WHAT DO YOU SAY TO THAT?
WOULD YOU CARE FOR A CUP OF TEA?

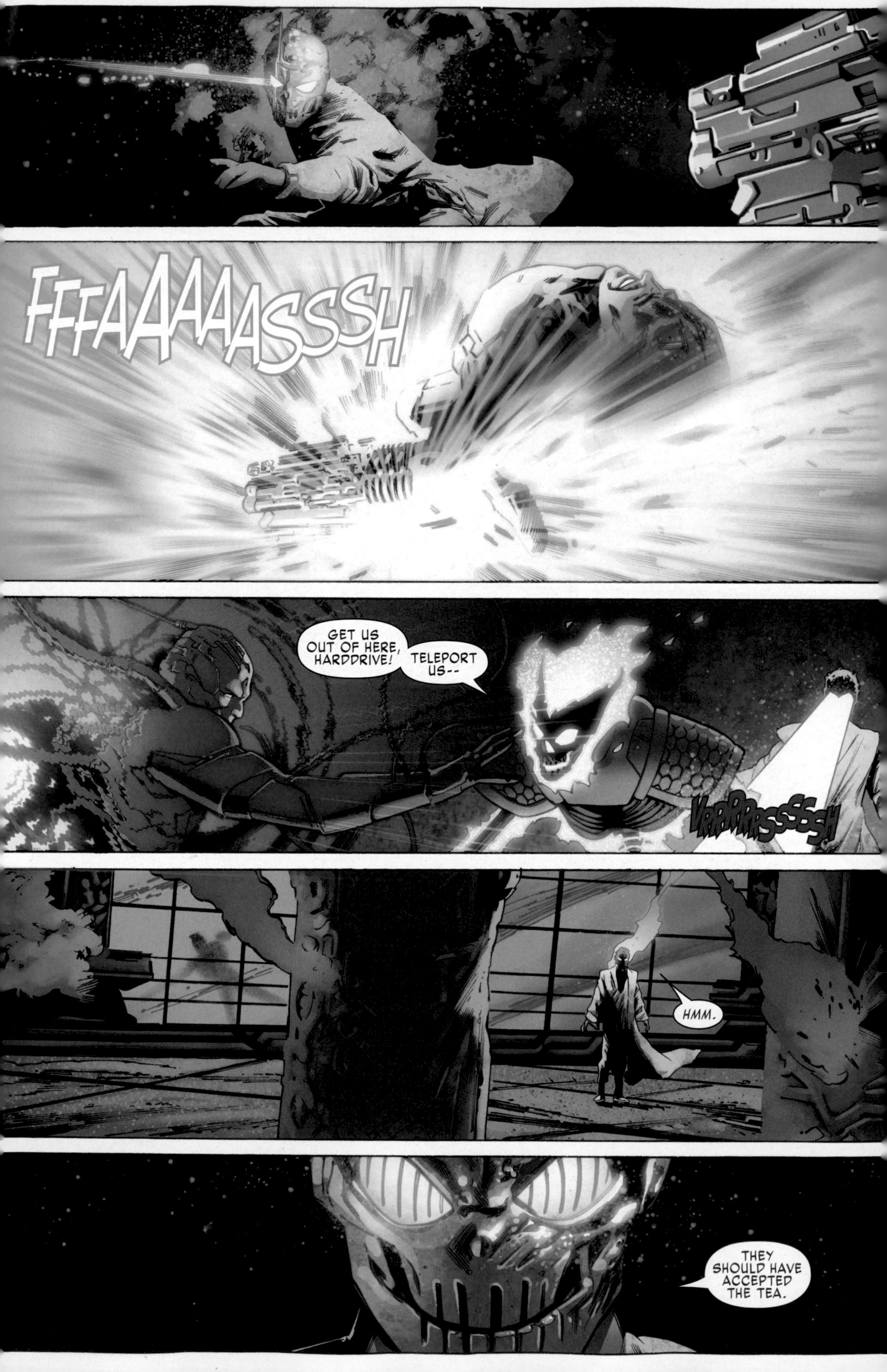
FFFAAAAASSSH
GET US OUT OF HERE, HARDDRIVE!
TELEPORT US--
VRRRRRSSSSSH
HMM.
THEY SHOULD HAVE ACCEPTED THE TEA.

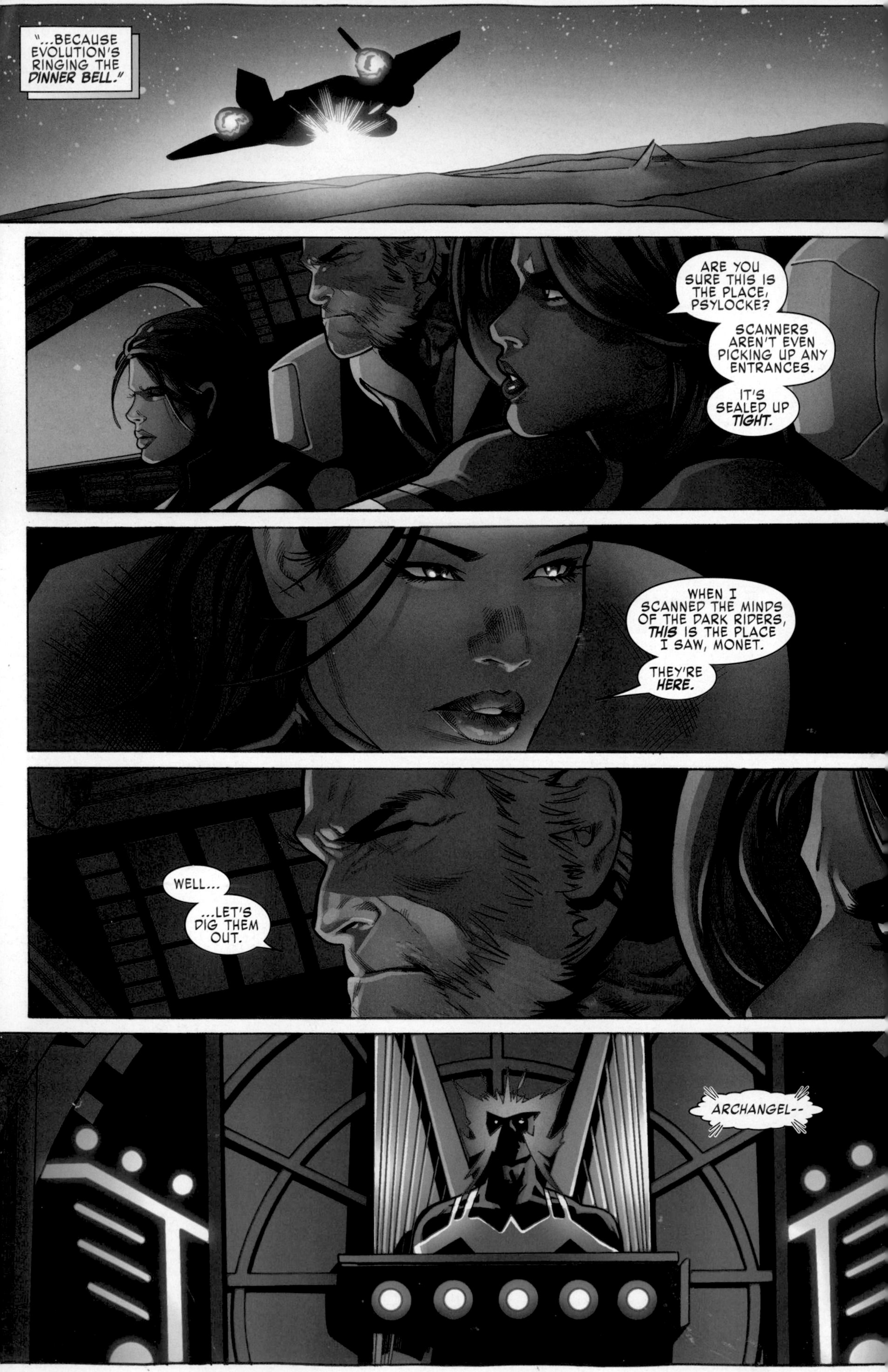
"...BECAUSE EVOLUTION'S RINGING THE DINNER BELL."
ARE YOU SURE THIS IS THE PLACE, PSYLOCKE?
SCANNERS AREN'T EVEN PICKING UP ANY ENTRANCES.
IT'S SEALED UP TIGHT.
WHEN I SCANNED THE MINDS OF THE DARK RIDERS, THIS IS THE PLACE I SAW, MONET.
THEY'RE HERE.
WELL...
...LET'S DIG THEM OUT.
ARCHANGEL--

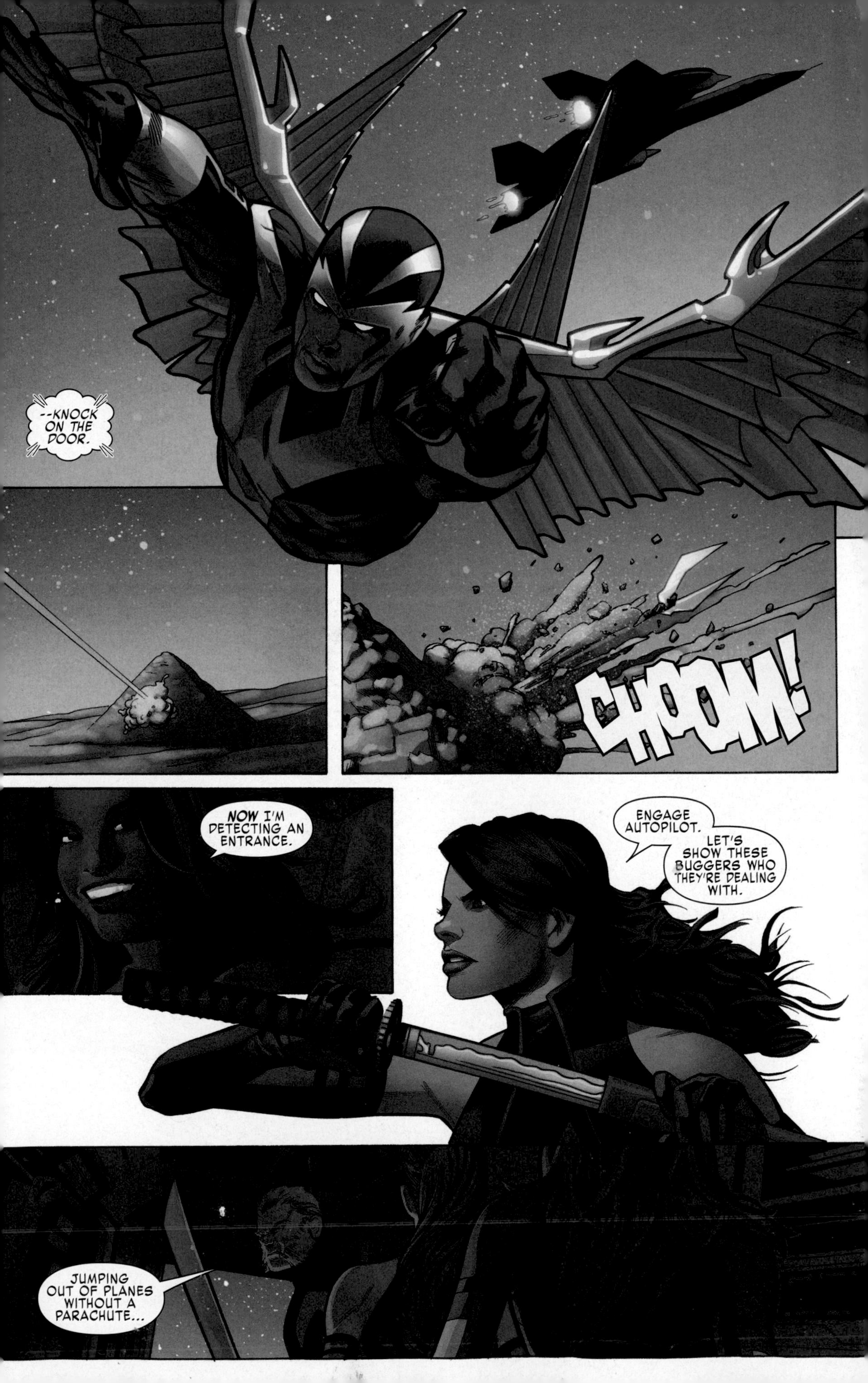
--KNOCK ON THE DOOR.
CHOOM!
NOW I'M DETECTING AN ENTRANCE.
ENGAGE AUTOPILOT.
LET'S SHOW THESE BUGGERS WHO THEY'RE DEALING WITH.
JUMPING OUT OF PLANES WITHOUT A PARACHUTE...

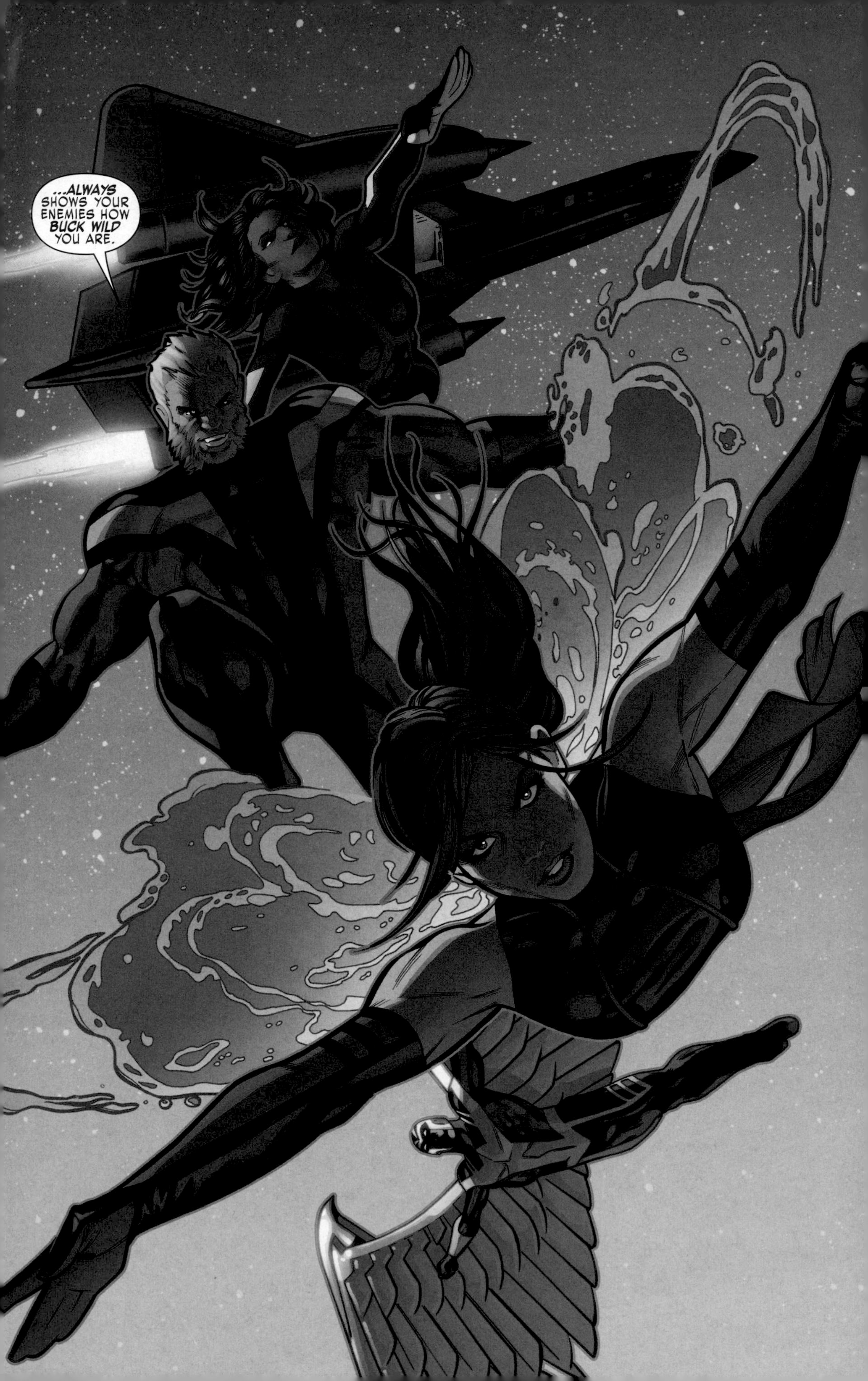
...ALWAYS SHOWS YOUR ENEMIES HOW BUCK WILD YOU ARE.

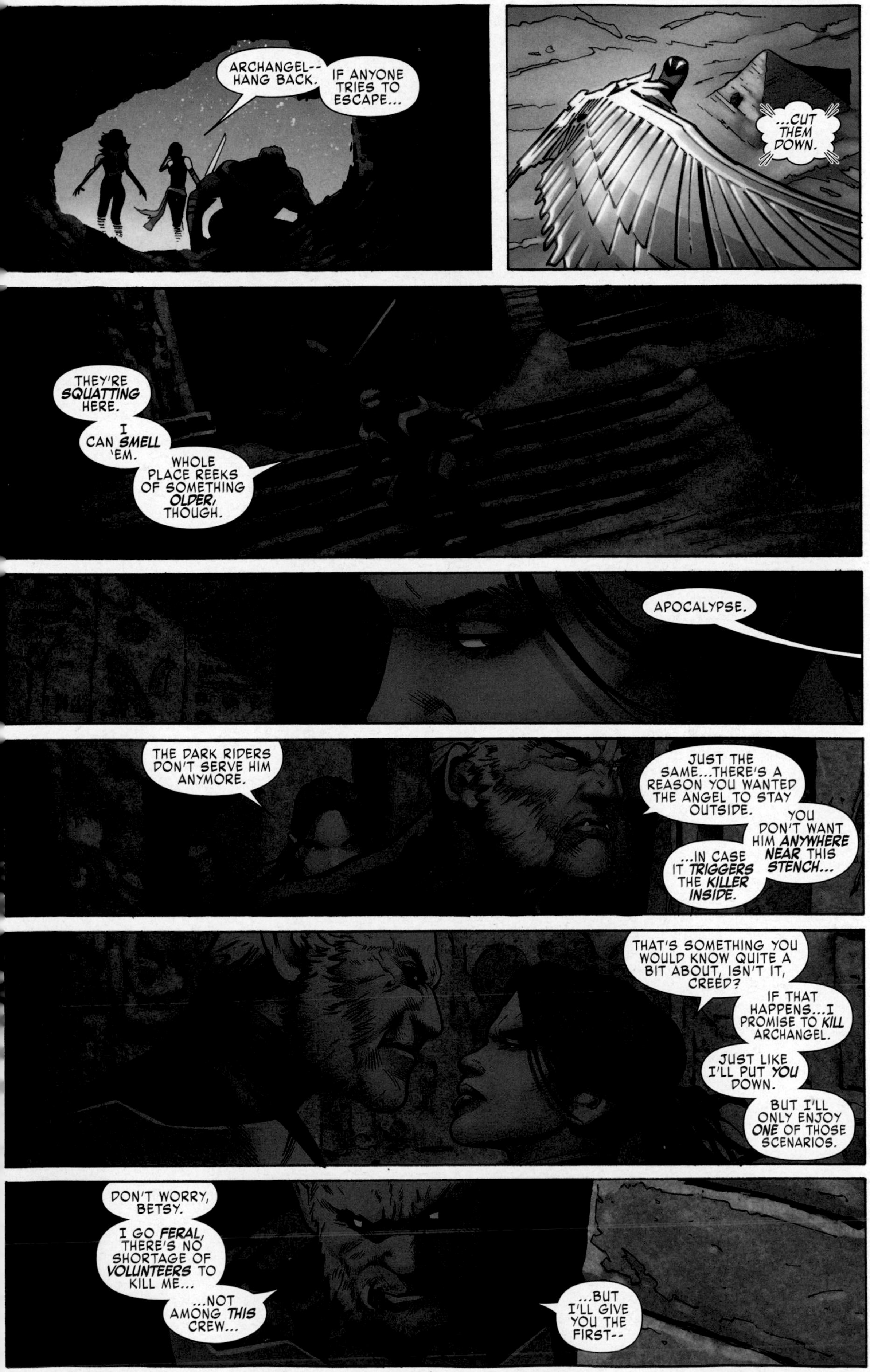
ARCHANGEL-- HANG BACK.
IF ANYONE TRIES TO ESCAPE...
...CUT THEM DOWN.
THEY'RE SQUATTING HERE.
I CAN SMELL 'EM.
WHOLE PLACE REEKS OF SOMETHING OLDER, THOUGH.
APOCALYPSE.
THE DARK RIDERS DON'T SERVE HIM ANYMORE.
JUST THE SAME...THERE'S A REASON YOU WANTED THE ANGEL TO STAY OUTSIDE.
YOU DON'T WANT HIM ANYWHERE NEAR THIS STENCH...
...IN CASE IT TRIGGERS THE KILLER INSIDE.
THAT'S SOMETHING YOU WOULD KNOW QUITE A BIT ABOUT, ISN'T IT, CREED?
IF THAT HAPPENS...I PROMISE TO KILL ARCHANGEL.
JUST LIKE I'LL PUT YOU DOWN.
BUT I'LL ONLY ENJOY ONE OF THOSE SCENARIOS.
DON'T WORRY, BETSY.
I GO FERAL, THERE'S NO SHORTAGE OF VOLUNTEERS TO KILL ME...
...NOT AMONG THIS CREW...
...BUT I'LL GIVE YOU THE FIRST--

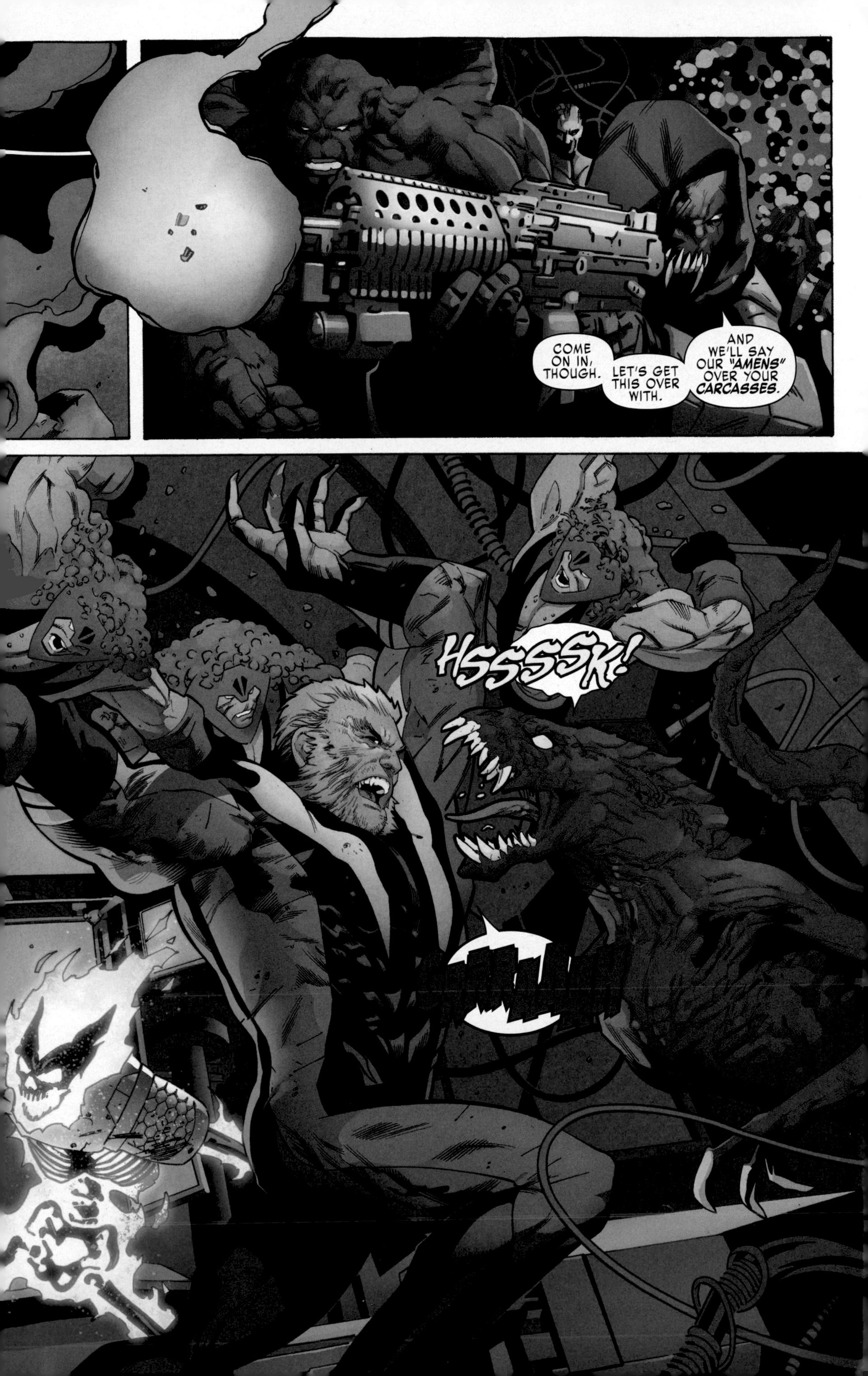
COME ON IN, THOUGH.
LET'S GET THIS OVER WITH.
AND WE'LL SAY OUR "AMENS" OVER YOUR CARCASSES.
HSSSSK!

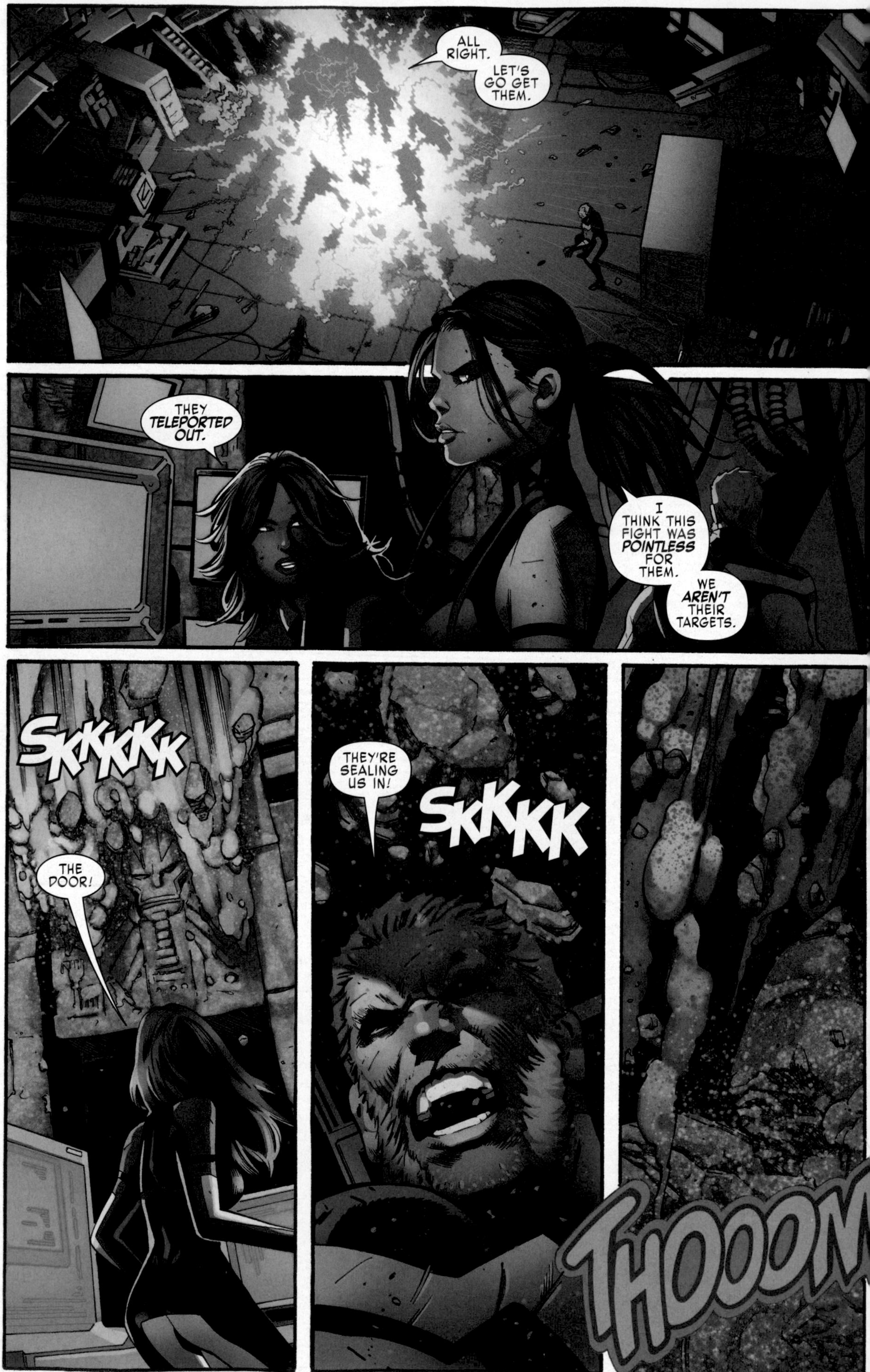
ALL RIGHT.
LET'S GO GET THEM.
THEY *TELEPORTED* OUT.
I THINK THIS FIGHT WAS *POINTLESS* FOR THEM.
WE *AREN'T* THEIR TARGETS.
SKKKKK
THE DOOR!
THEY'RE SEALING US IN!
SKKKK
THOOOM

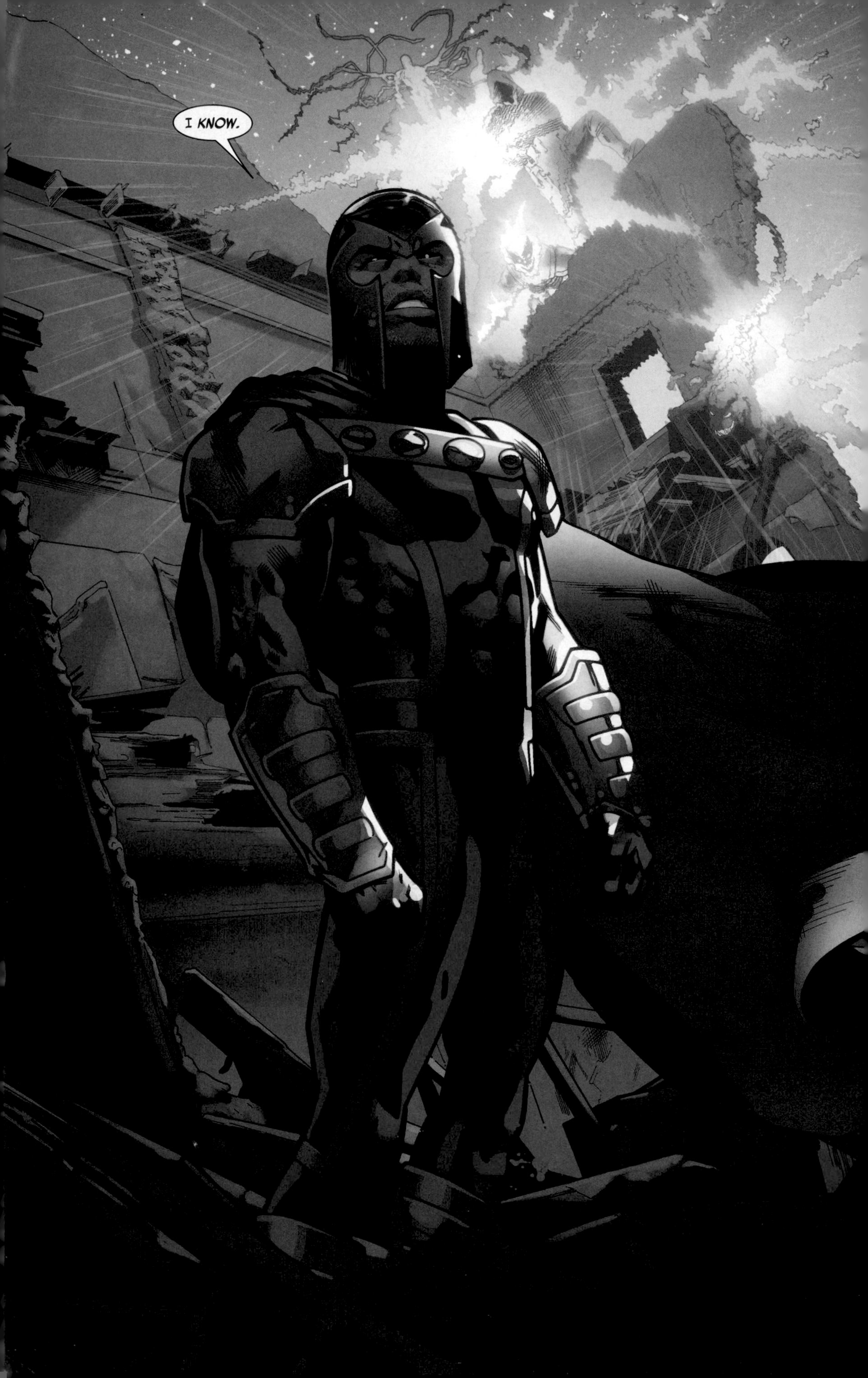
I KNOW.

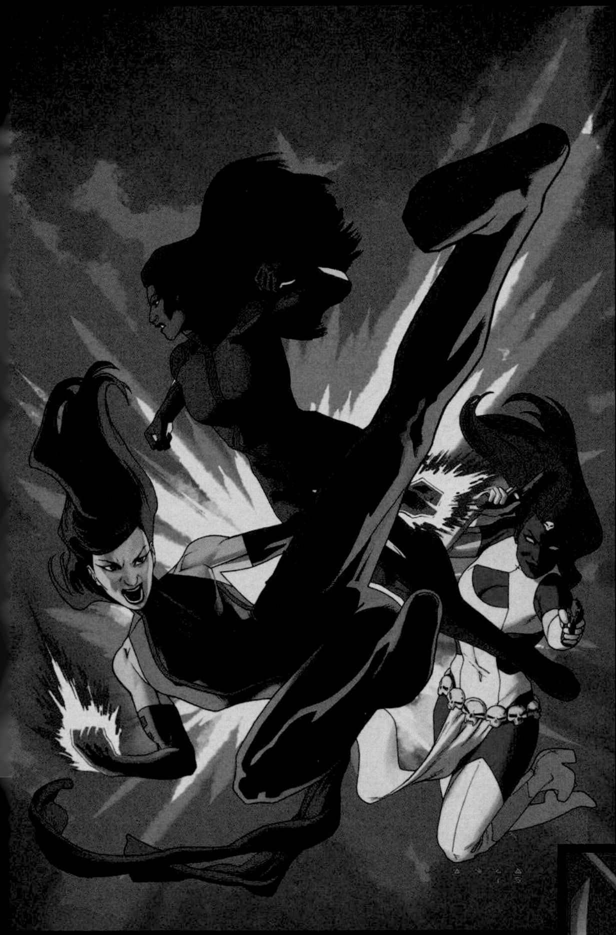

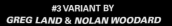

#2 VARIANT BY
KRIS ANKA

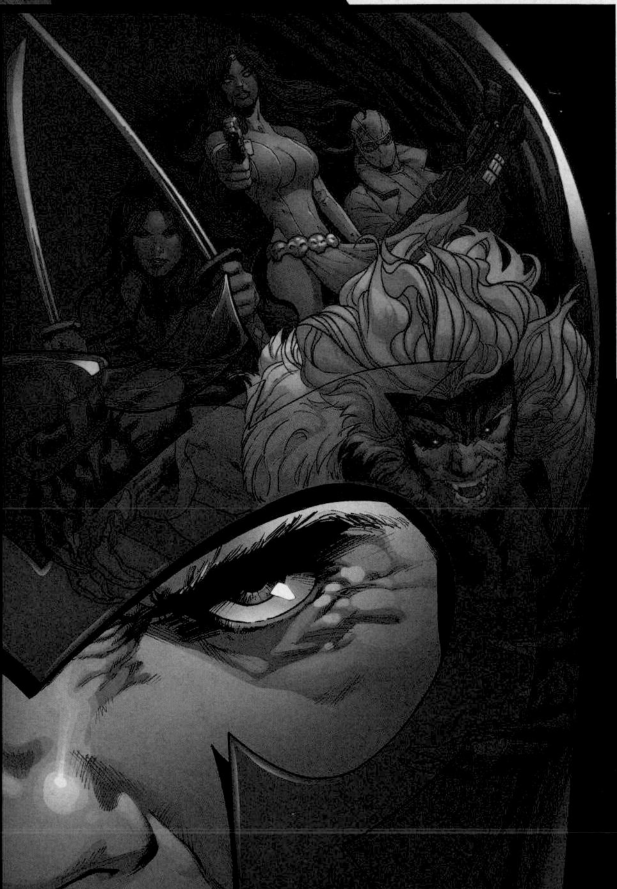

#3 VARIANT BY
GREG LAND & NOLAN WOODARD

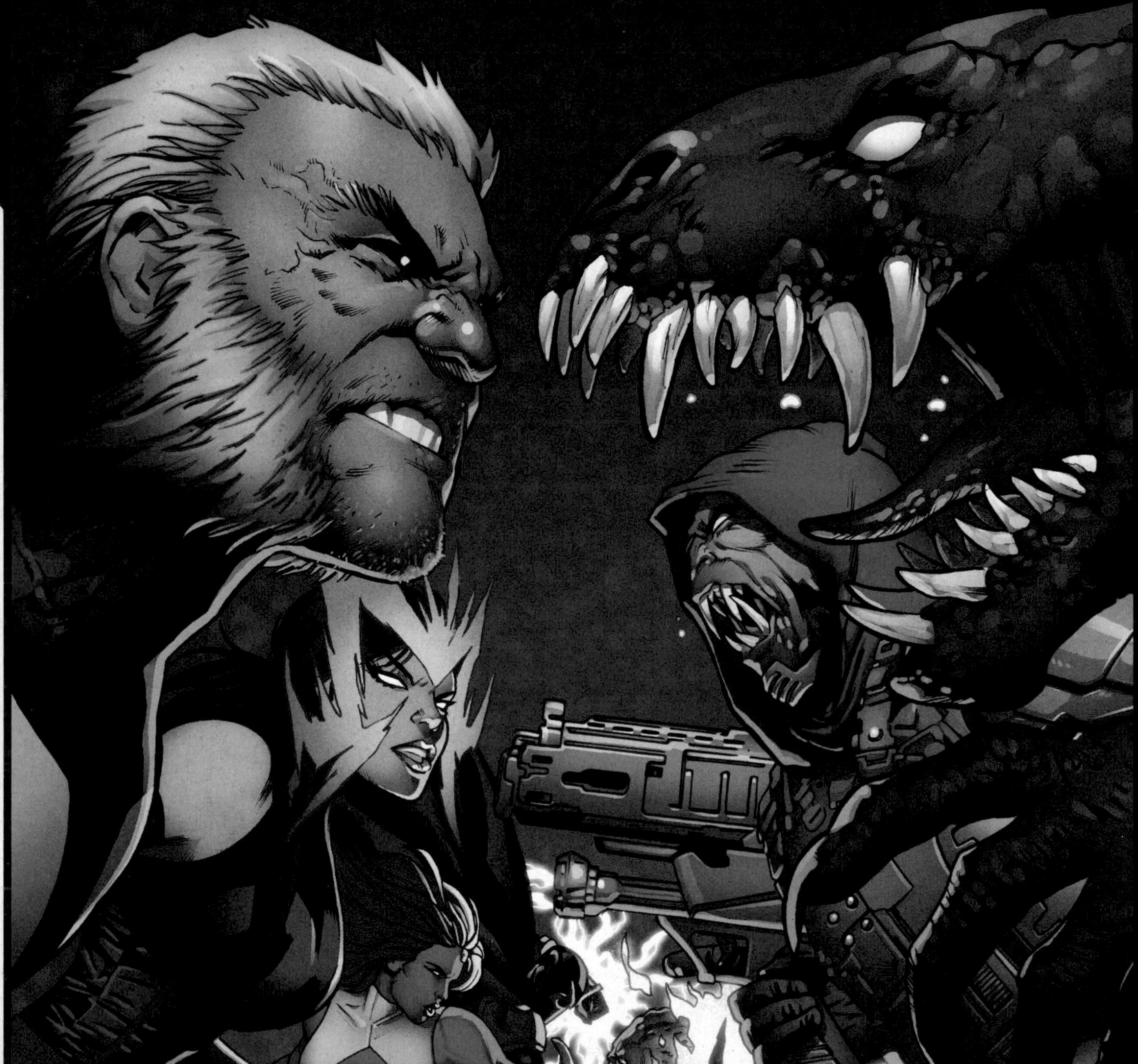

5

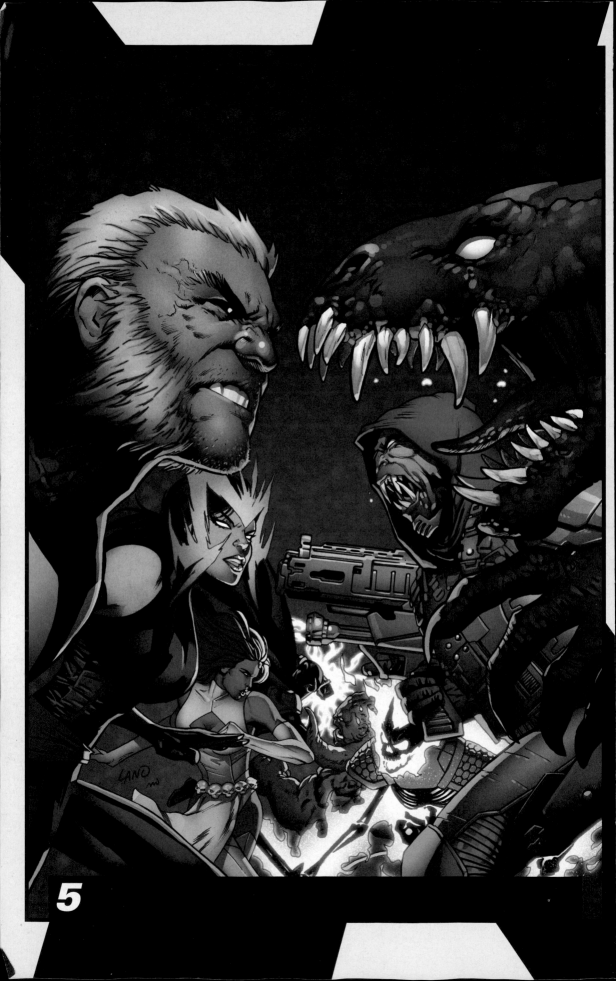

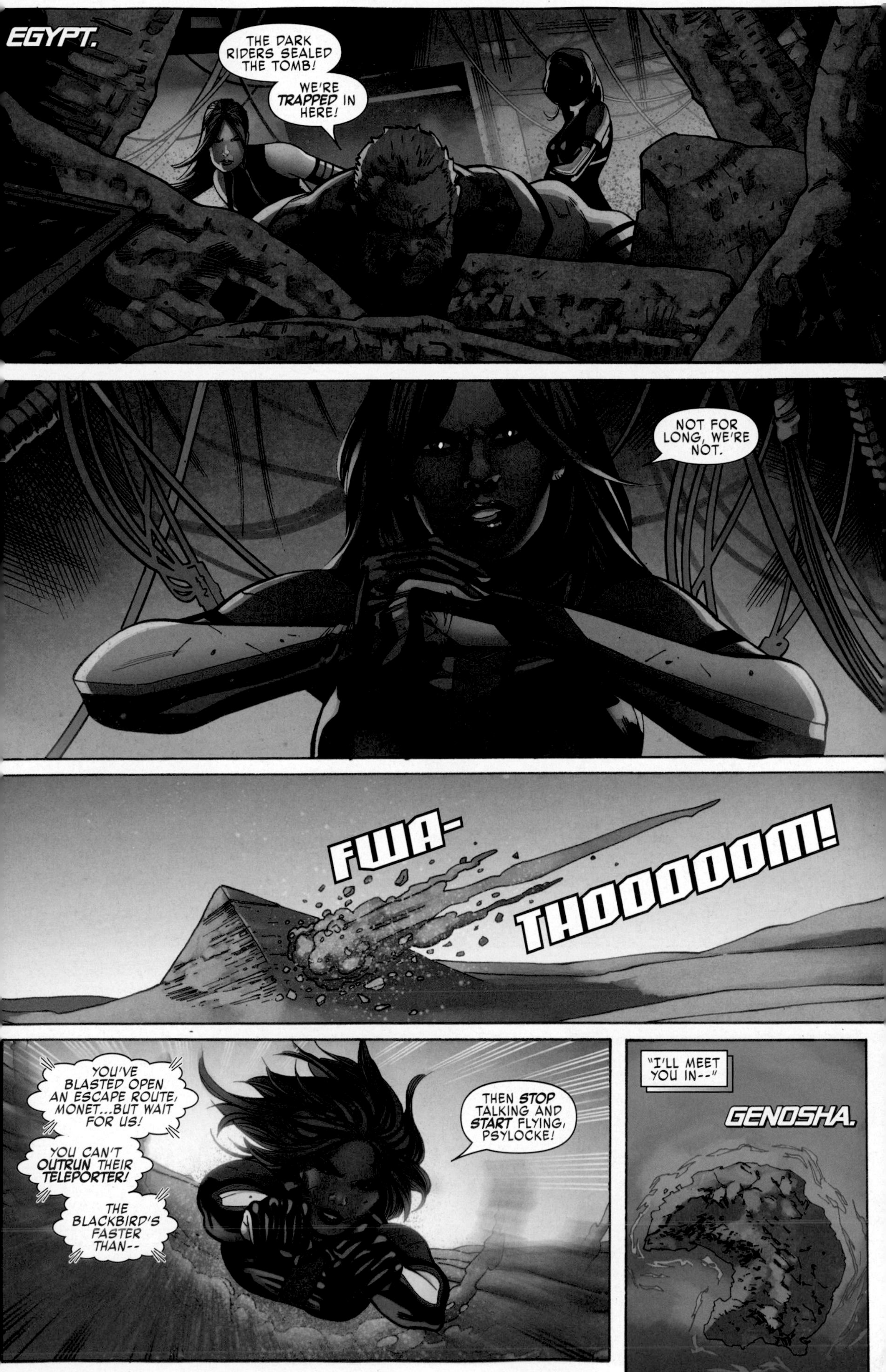
EGYPT.
THE DARK RIDERS SEALED THE TOMB!
WE'RE TRAPPED IN HERE!
NOT FOR LONG, WE'RE NOT.
FWA-THOOOOOOM!
YOU'VE BLASTED OPEN AN ESCAPE ROUTE, MONET...BUT WAIT FOR US!
YOU CAN'T OUTRUN THEIR TELEPORTER!
THE BLACKBIRD'S FASTER THAN--
THEN STOP TALKING AND START FLYING, PSYLOCKE!
"I'LL MEET YOU IN--"
GENOSHA.

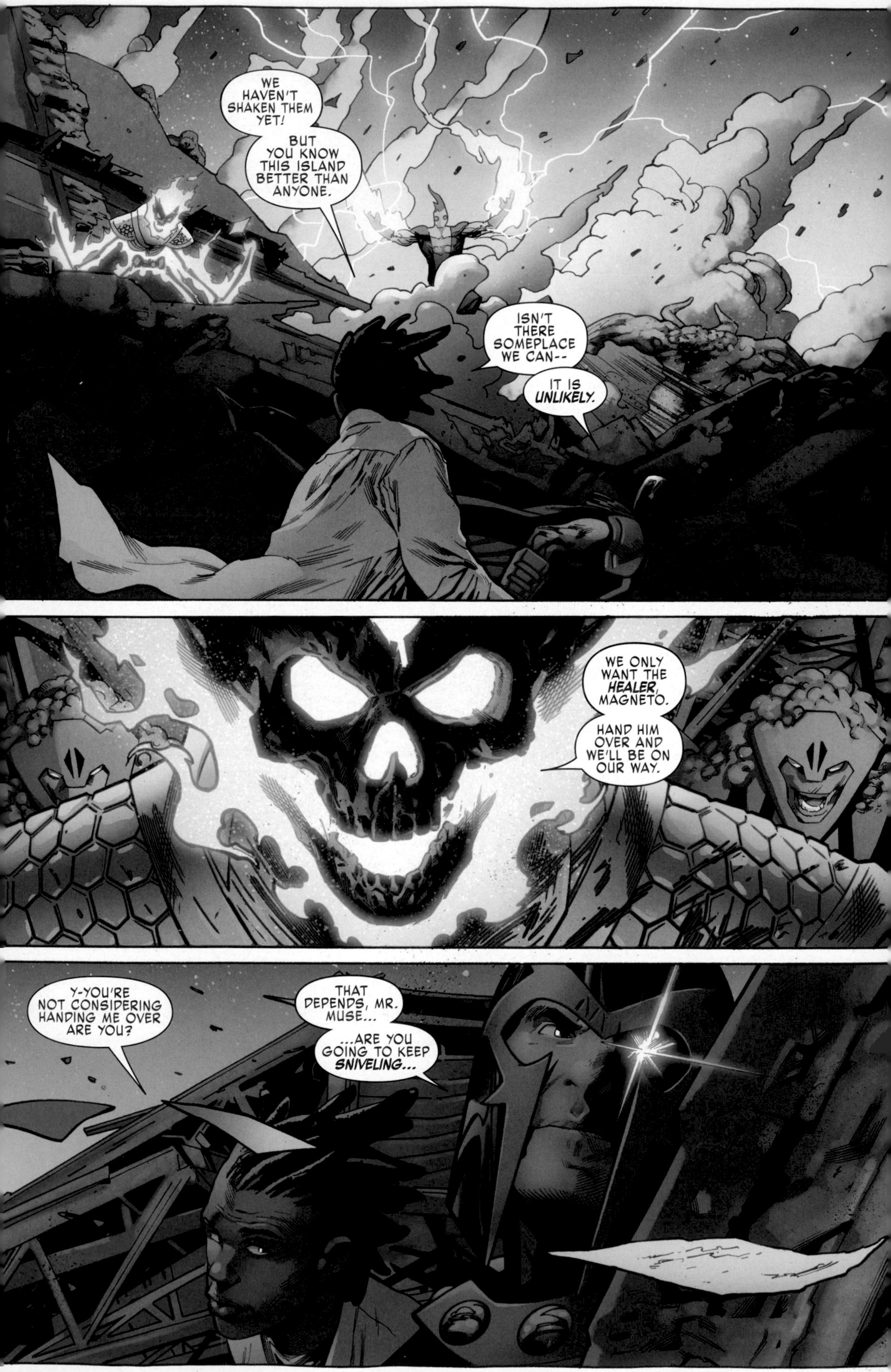
WE HAVEN'T SHAKEN THEM YET!
BUT YOU KNOW THIS ISLAND BETTER THAN ANYONE.
ISN'T THERE SOMEPLACE WE CAN--
IT IS *UNLIKELY.*
WE ONLY WANT THE *HEALER*, MAGNETO.
HAND HIM OVER AND WE'LL BE ON OUR WAY.
Y-YOU'RE NOT CONSIDERING HANDING ME OVER ARE YOU?
THAT DEPENDS, MR. MUSE...
...ARE YOU GOING TO KEEP *SNIVELING...*

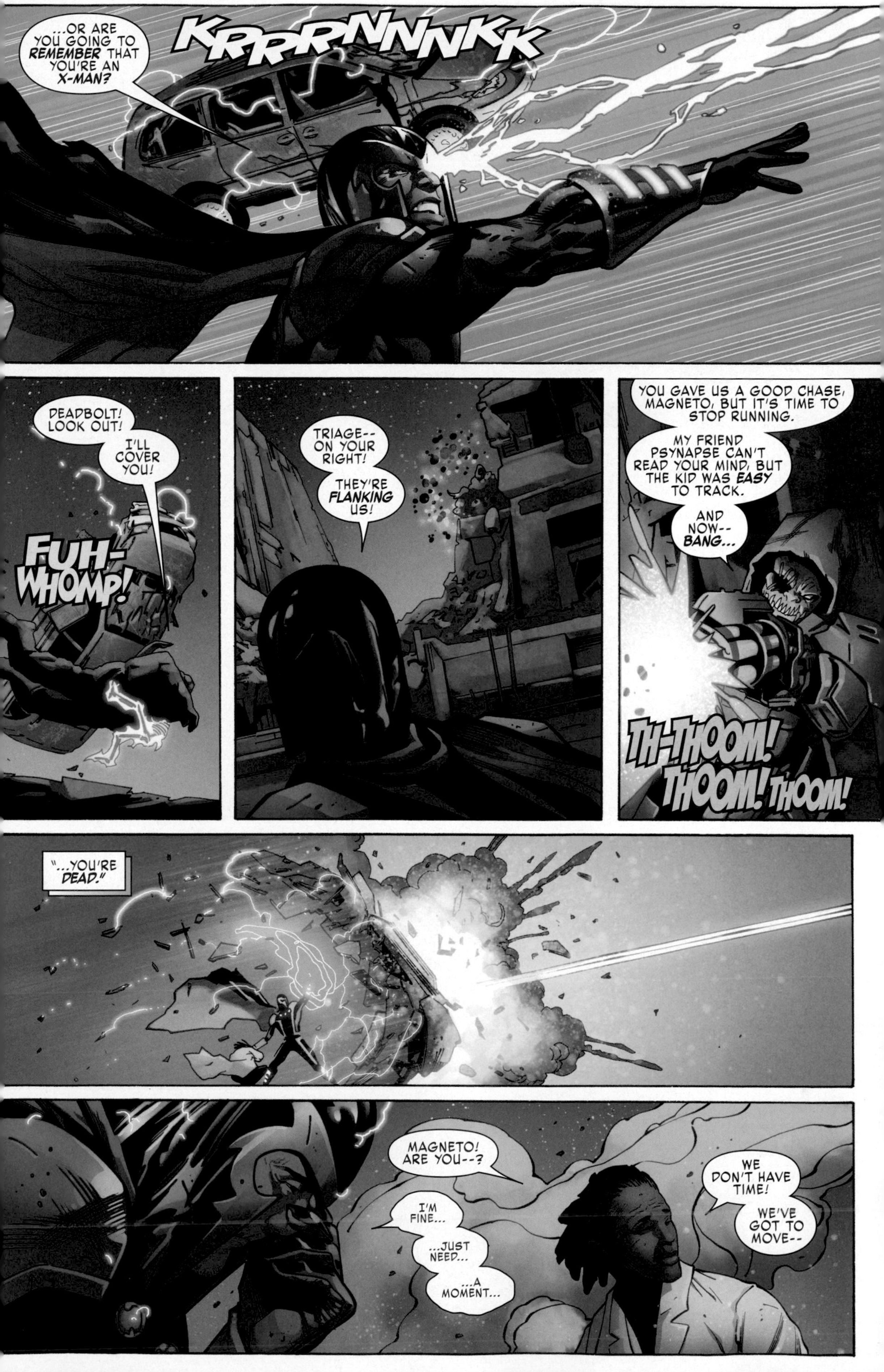
...OR ARE YOU GOING TO REMEMBER THAT YOU'RE AN X-MAN?
KRRRNNNKK
DEADBOLT! LOOK OUT!
I'LL COVER YOU!
FUH-WHOMP!
TRIAGE-- ON YOUR RIGHT!
THEY'RE FLANKING US!
YOU GAVE US A GOOD CHASE, MAGNETO, BUT IT'S TIME TO STOP RUNNING.
MY FRIEND PSYNAPSE CAN'T READ YOUR MIND, BUT THE KID WAS EASY TO TRACK.
AND NOW-- BANG...
TH-THOOM! THOOM! THOOM!
"...YOU'RE DEAD."
MAGNETO! ARE YOU--?
I'M FINE...
...JUST NEED...
...A MOMENT...
WE DON'T HAVE TIME!
WE'VE GOT TO MOVE--

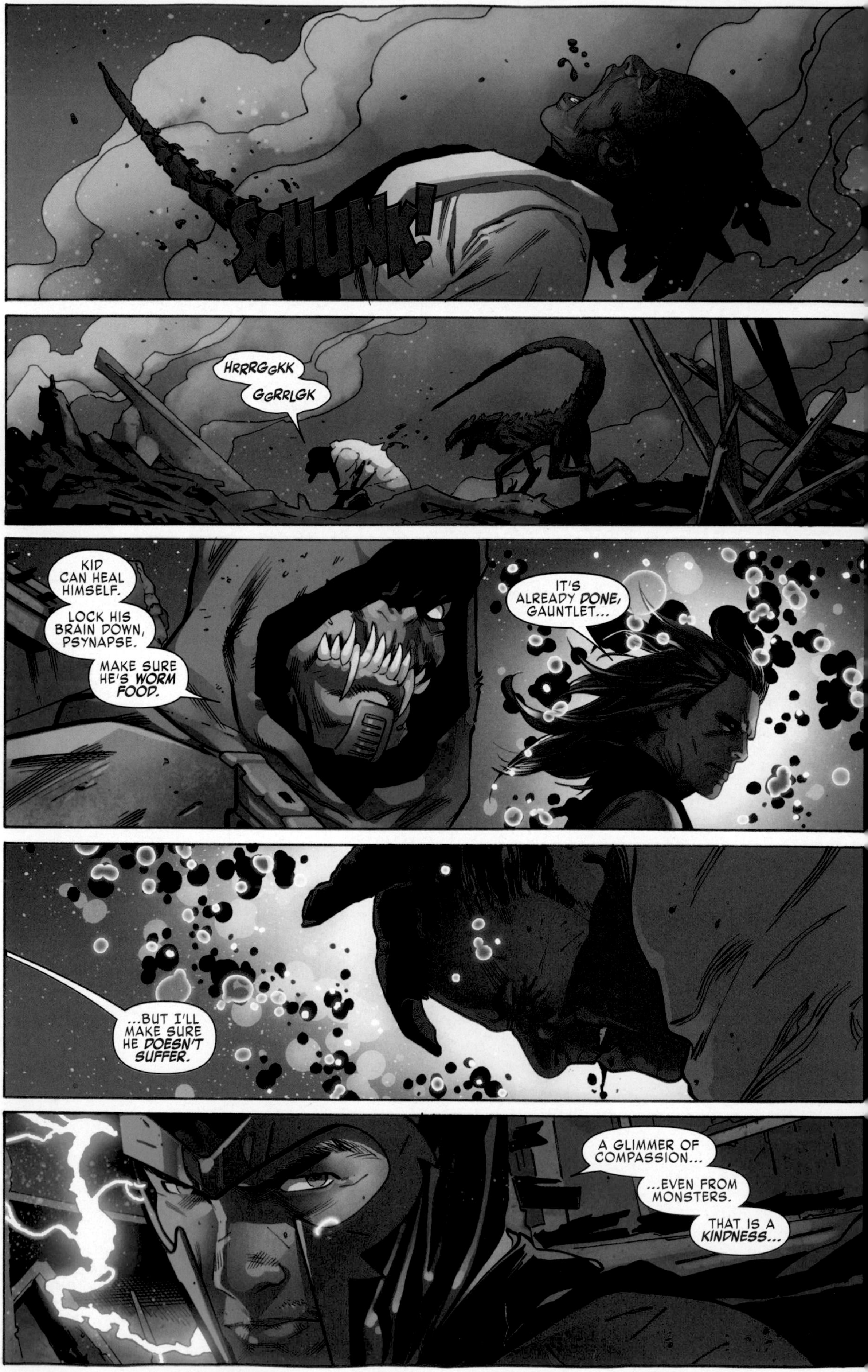
SCHUNK!
HRRRGGKK
GGRRLGK
KID CAN HEAL HIMSELF.
LOCK HIS BRAIN DOWN, PSYNAPSE.
MAKE SURE HE'S WORM FOOD.
IT'S ALREADY DONE, GAUNTLET...
...BUT I'LL MAKE SURE HE DOESN'T SUFFER.
A GLIMMER OF COMPASSION...
...EVEN FROM MONSTERS.
THAT IS A KINDNESS...

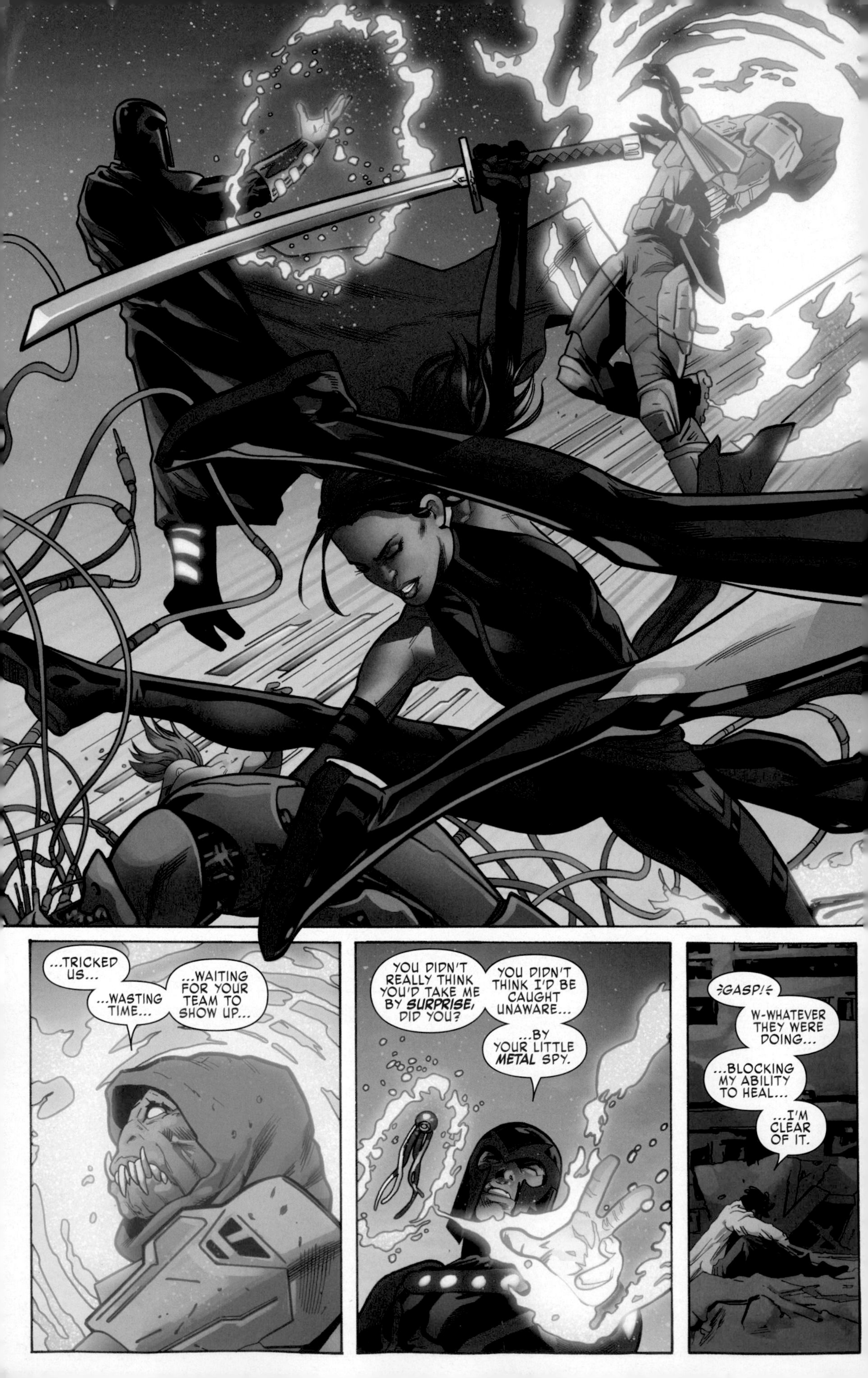
...TRICKED US...
...WASTING TIME...
...WAITING FOR YOUR TEAM TO SHOW UP...
YOU DIDN'T REALLY THINK YOU'D TAKE ME BY SURPRISE, DID YOU?
YOU DIDN'T THINK I'D BE CAUGHT UNAWARE...
...BY YOUR LITTLE METAL SPY.
GASP!
W-WHATEVER THEY WERE DOING...
...BLOCKING MY ABILITY TO HEAL...
...I'M CLEAR OF IT.

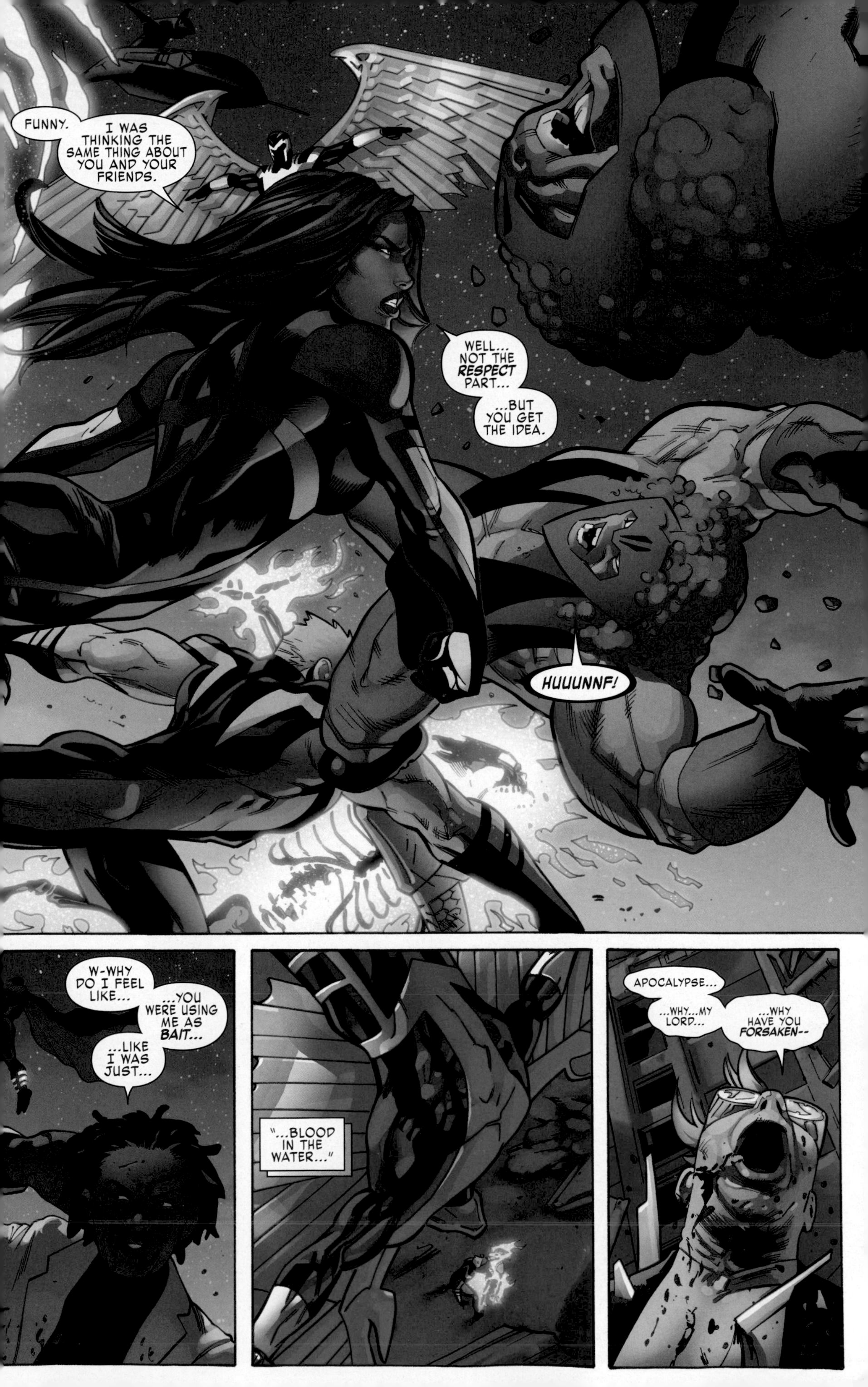
FUNNY.
I WAS THINKING THE SAME THING ABOUT YOU AND YOUR FRIENDS.
WELL... NOT THE RESPECT PART...
...BUT YOU GET THE IDEA.
HUUUNNF!
W-WHY DO I FEEL LIKE...
...YOU WERE USING ME AS BAIT...
...LIKE I WAS JUST...
"...BLOOD IN THE WATER..."
APOCALYPSE...
...WHY...MY LORD...
...WHY HAVE YOU FORSAKEN--

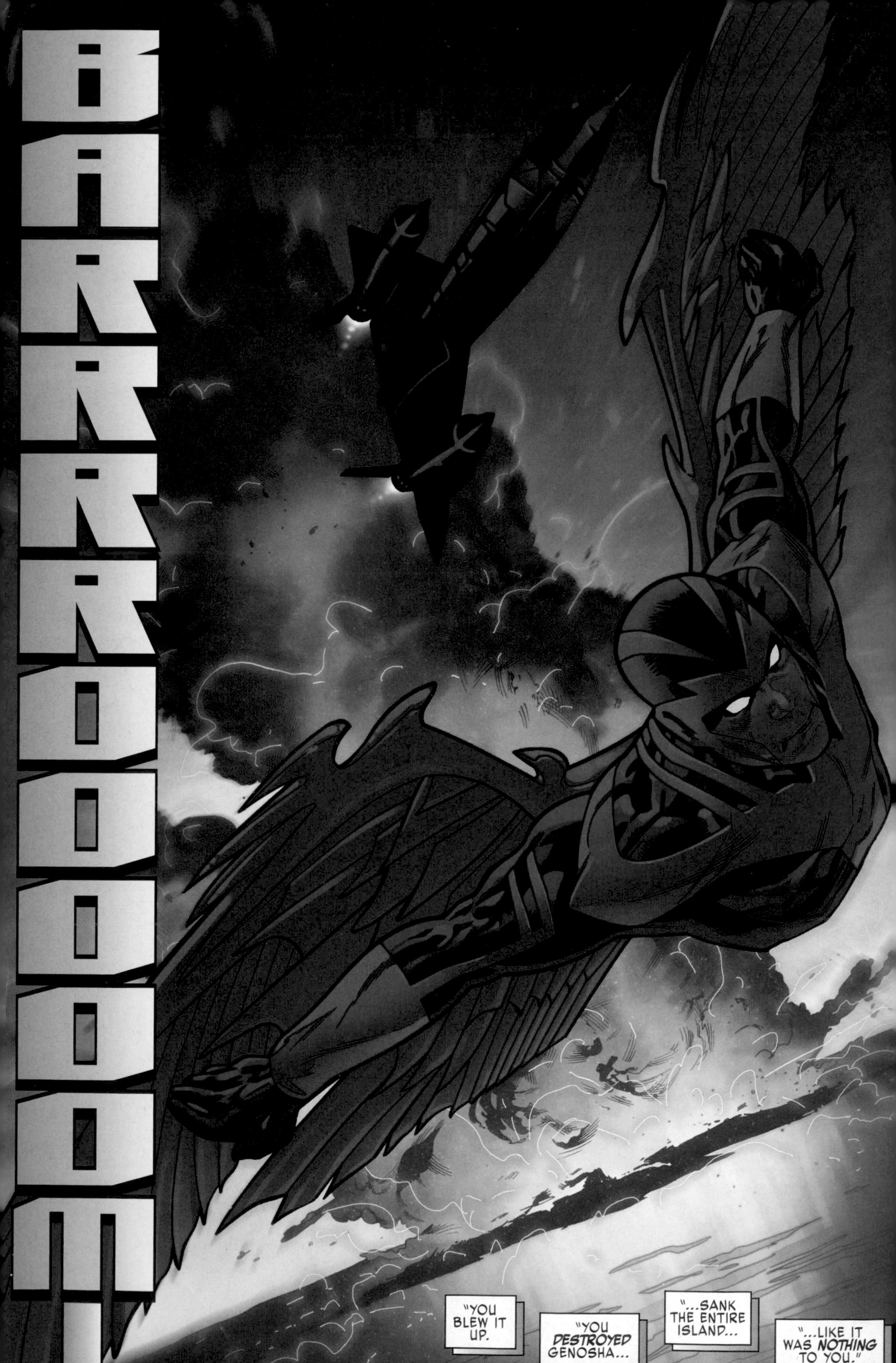
BARROOOM!
"YOU BLEW IT UP.
"YOU **DESTROYED** GENOSHA...
"...SANK THE ENTIRE ISLAND...
"...LIKE IT WAS **NOTHING** TO YOU."

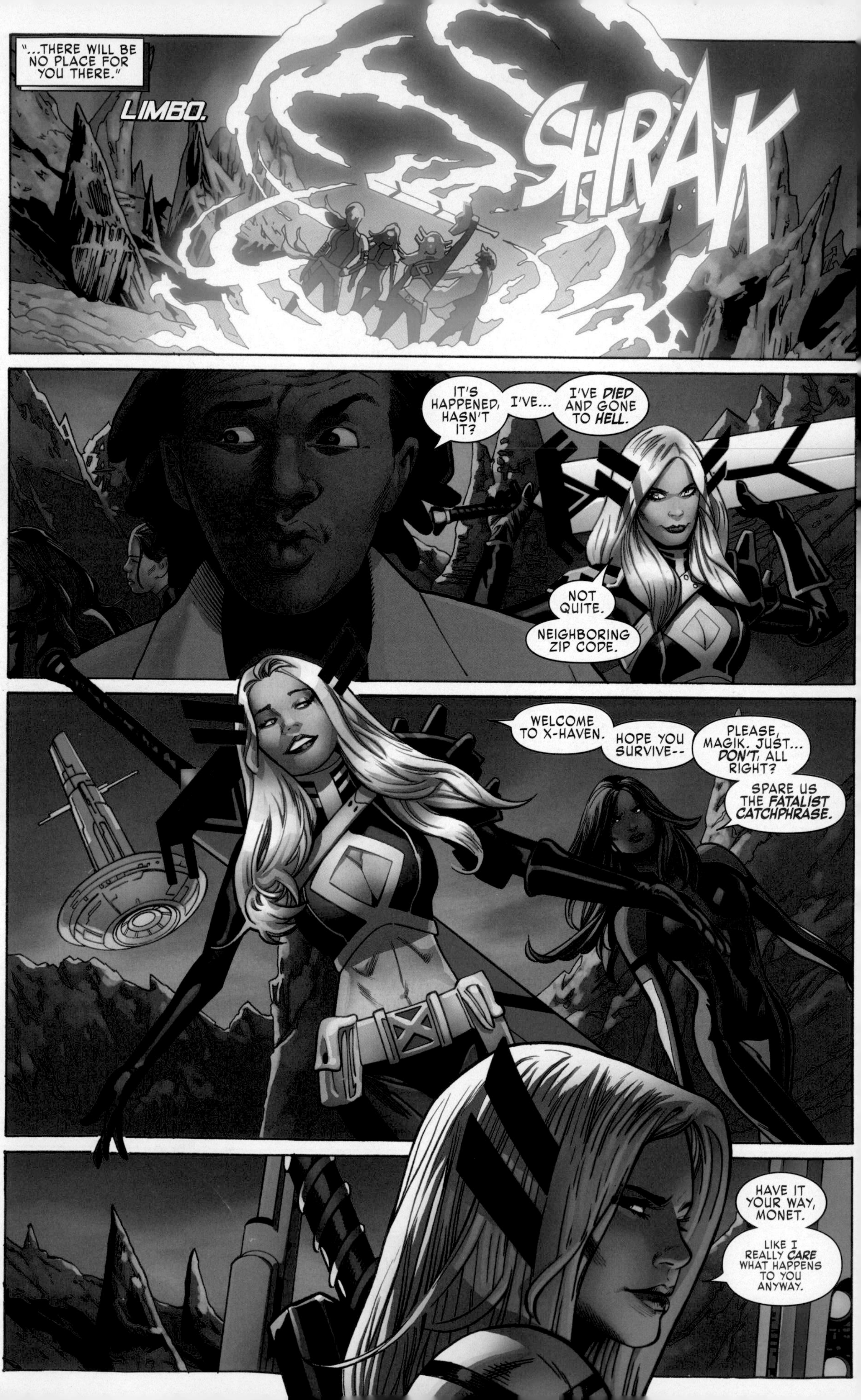
"...THERE WILL BE NO PLACE FOR YOU THERE."
LIMBO.
SHRAK
IT'S HAPPENED, HASN'T IT?
I'VE...
I'VE DIED AND GONE TO HELL.
NOT QUITE.
NEIGHBORING ZIP CODE.
WELCOME TO X-HAVEN.
HOPE YOU SURVIVE--
PLEASE, MAGIK. JUST... DON'T, ALL RIGHT?
SPARE US THE FATALIST CATCHPHRASE.
HAVE IT YOUR WAY, MONET.
LIKE I REALLY CARE WHAT HAPPENS TO YOU ANYWAY.

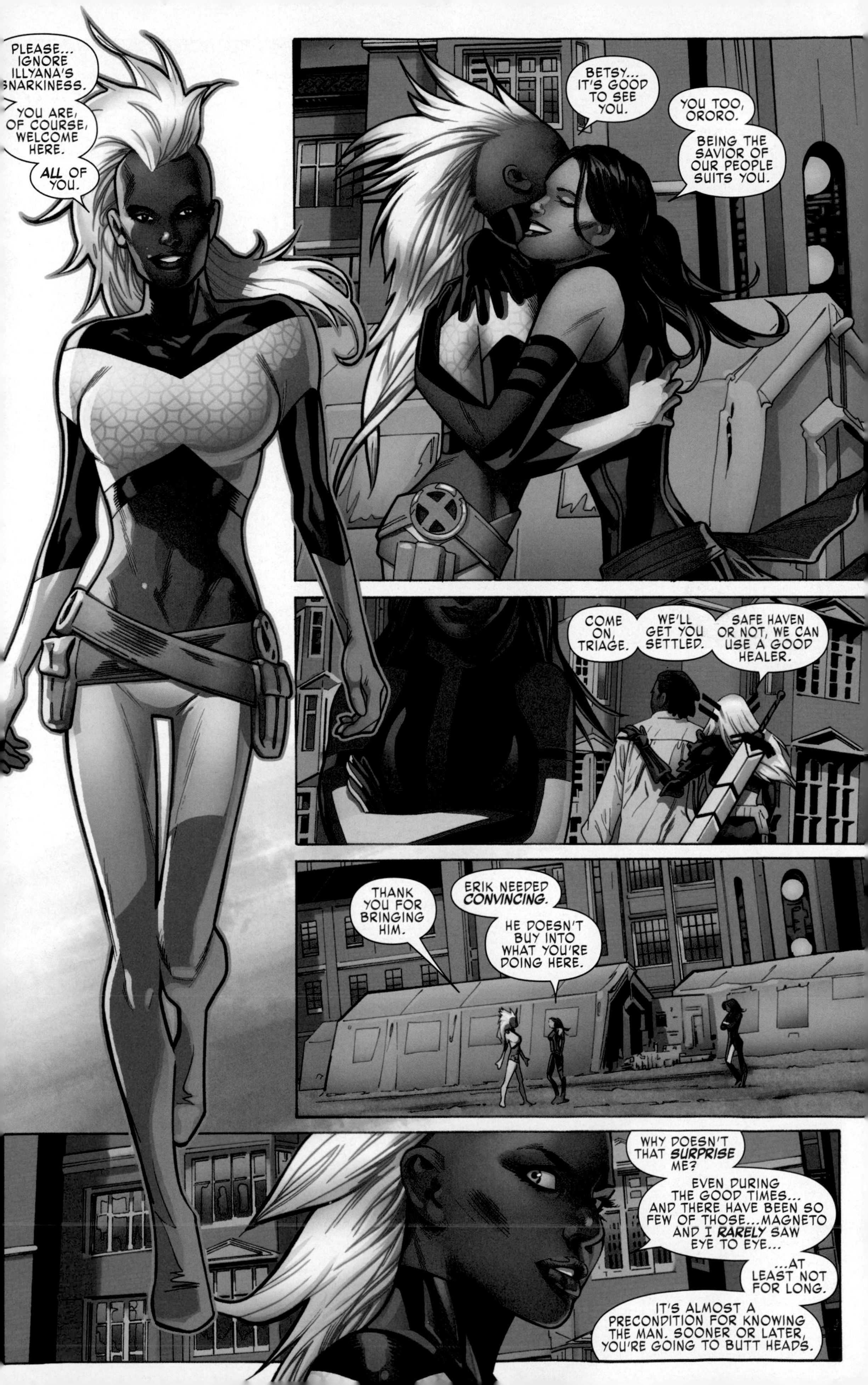

PLEASE... IGNORE ILLYANA'S SNARKINESS.
YOU ARE, OF COURSE, WELCOME HERE.
ALL OF YOU.
BETSY... IT'S GOOD TO SEE YOU.
YOU TOO, ORORO.
BEING THE SAVIOR OF OUR PEOPLE SUITS YOU.
COME ON, TRIAGE.
WE'LL GET YOU SETTLED.
SAFE HAVEN OR NOT, WE CAN USE A GOOD HEALER.
THANK YOU FOR BRINGING HIM.
ERIK NEEDED *CONVINCING*.
HE DOESN'T BUY INTO WHAT YOU'RE DOING HERE.
WHY DOESN'T THAT *SURPRISE* ME?
EVEN DURING THE GOOD TIMES... AND THERE HAVE BEEN SO FEW OF THOSE...MAGNETO AND I *RARELY* SAW EYE TO EYE...
...AT LEAST NOT FOR LONG.
IT'S ALMOST A PRECONDITION FOR KNOWING THE MAN. SOONER OR LATER, YOU'RE GOING TO BUTT HEADS.

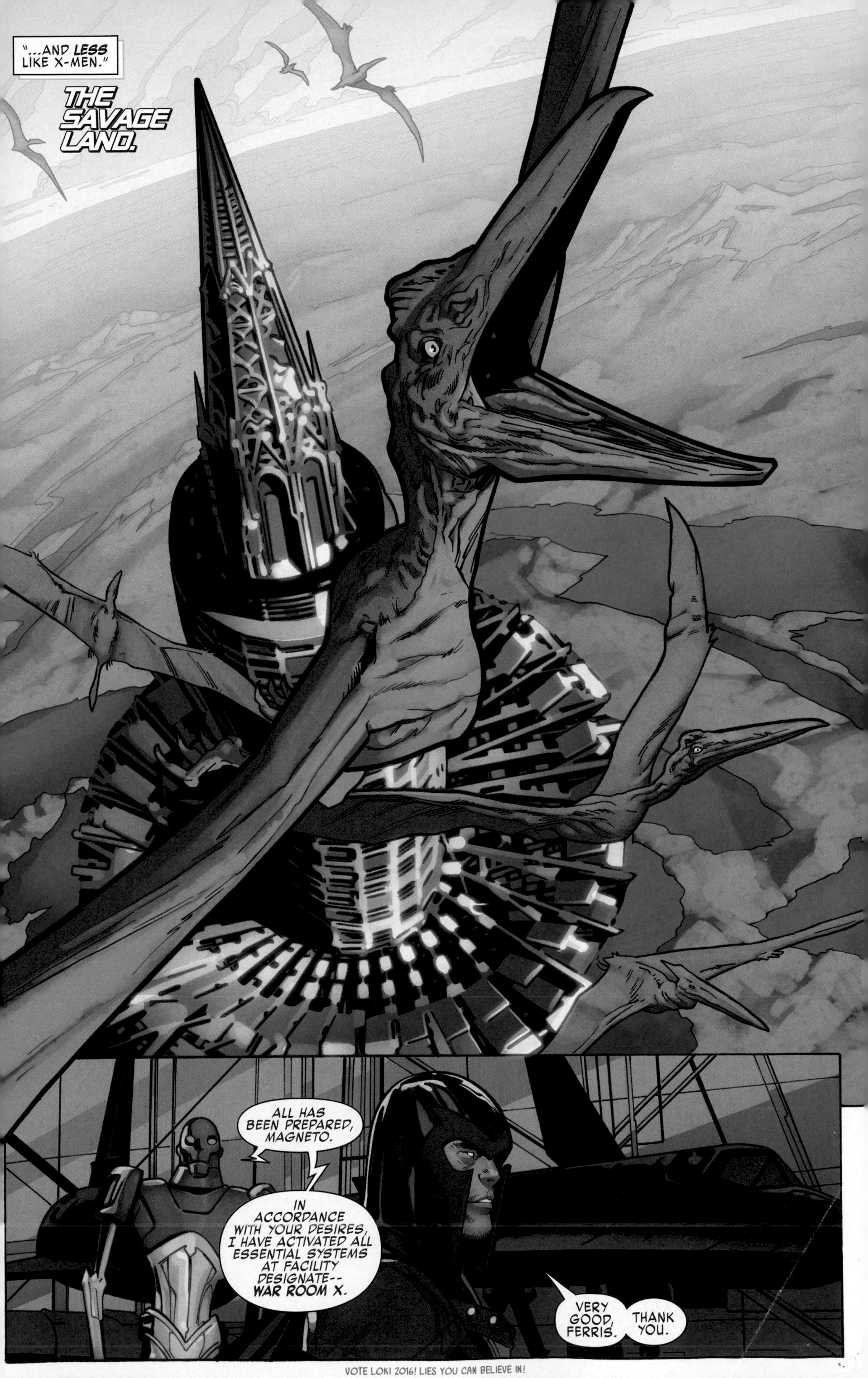
"...AND LESS LIKE X-MEN."
THE SAVAGE LAND.
ALL HAS BEEN PREPARED, MAGNETO.
IN ACCORDANCE WITH YOUR DESIRES, I HAVE ACTIVATED ALL ESSENTIAL SYSTEMS AT FACILITY DESIGNATE-- WAR ROOM X.
VERY GOOD, FERRIS.
THANK YOU.

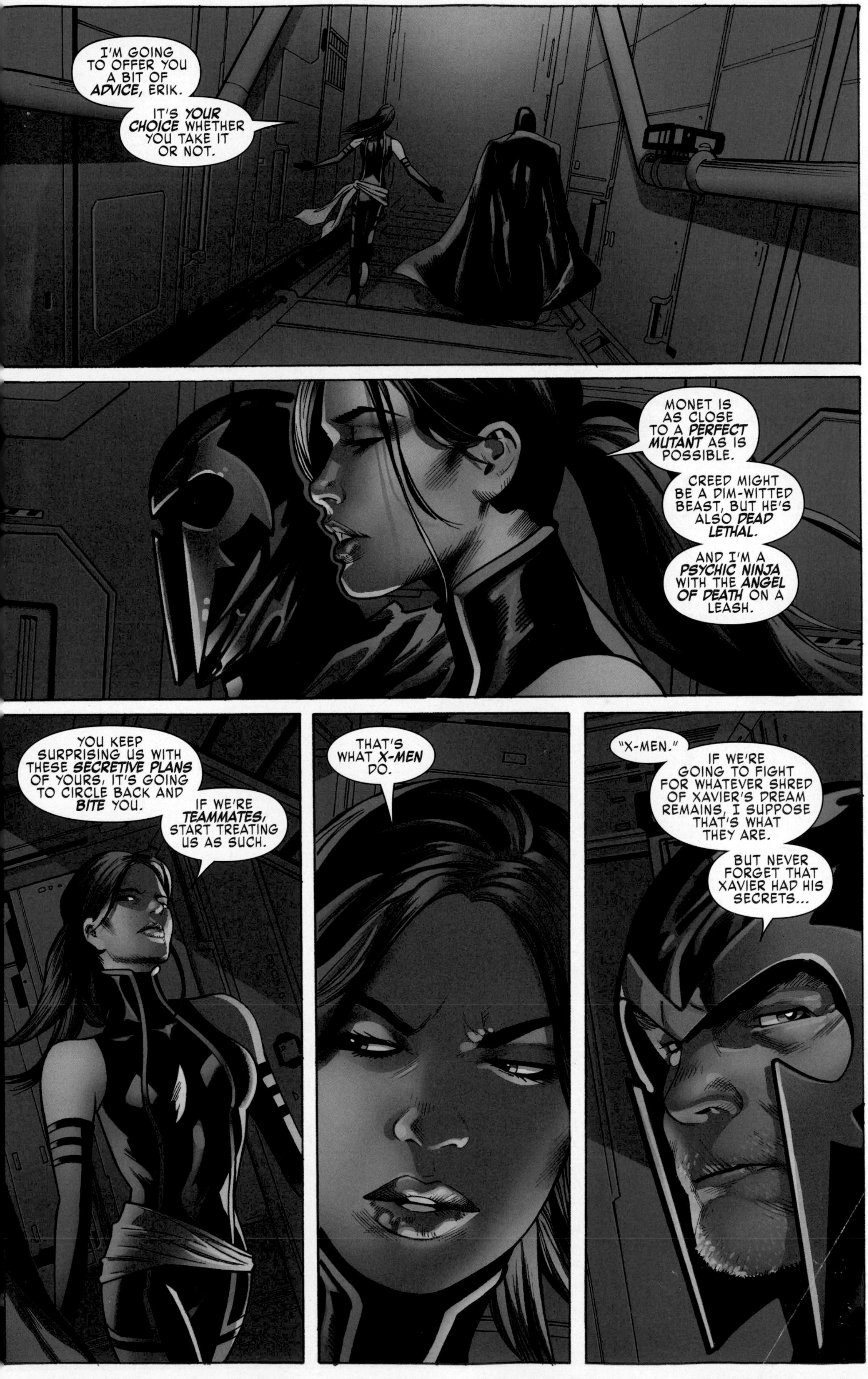
I'M GOING TO OFFER YOU A BIT OF ADVICE, ERIK.
IT'S YOUR CHOICE WHETHER YOU TAKE IT OR NOT.
MONET IS AS CLOSE TO A PERFECT MUTANT AS IS POSSIBLE.
CREED MIGHT BE A DIM-WITTED BEAST, BUT HE'S ALSO DEAD LETHAL.
AND I'M A PSYCHIC NINJA WITH THE ANGEL OF DEATH ON A LEASH.
YOU KEEP SURPRISING US WITH THESE SECRETIVE PLANS OF YOURS, IT'S GOING TO CIRCLE BACK AND BITE YOU.
IF WE'RE TEAMMATES, START TREATING US AS SUCH.
THAT'S WHAT X-MEN DO.
"X-MEN."
IF WE'RE GOING TO FIGHT FOR WHATEVER SHRED OF XAVIER'S DREAM REMAINS, I SUPPOSE THAT'S WHAT THEY ARE.
BUT NEVER FORGET THAT XAVIER HAD HIS SECRETS...

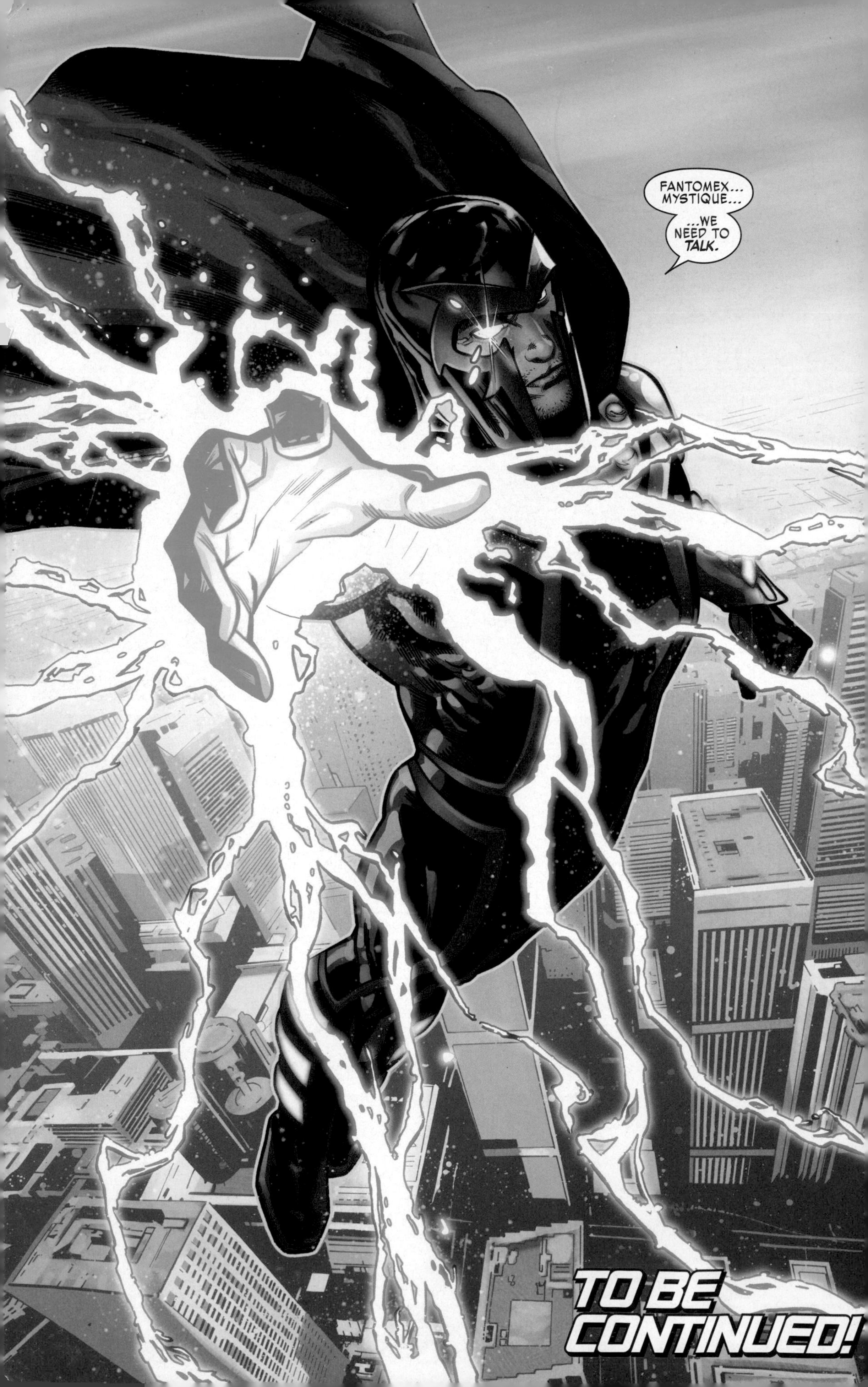
FANTOMEX... MYSTIQUE...
...WE NEED TO TALK.
TO BE CONTINUED!